UNSCREWED

"Retirement Secrets Wall Street Prays You Never Learn"

Barry Harrin & Raymond Leeper
Published By Comanche Press

Other Books from Comanche Press:

FIRST EDITION
Copyright © 2013
By Barry Harrin & Raymond Leeper
Published in the United States of America
By Comanche Press
906 Lightstone Drive, San Antonio Texas 78258
Email: comanchepress@gmail.com
Websites: www.harringroup.com and www.leeperllp.com

ALL RIGHTS RESERVED
ISBN: 978-0-9626012-8-6
Library of Congress Catalog Control Number: 2013916011

DEDICATION

This book is dedicated to the late Paul Leeper, founder of the Leeper Group LLP. His professionalism; and his love of his family, friends and clients will live on. The information in this book was the information he shared with us. He was always fascinated by the myriad of ways life insurance could benefit people.

Paul taught us that applied knowledge always trumped theory. He taught us that "people don't care how much you know until they know how much you care." He carefully planned the transfer of his assets upon his death and applied many of the concepts in this book with not only his clients but for himself as well. He believed in what he sold and sold what he believed in.

"The best way to help poor people is not to be one of them."

-Paul Leeper

Table of Contents

PREFACE

Our intention in writing this book is to help the average middle class American win the retirement game. If you are in the middle class, you know in your heart the game is rigged ... and not in your favor.

We are going to identify common mistakes to avoid. Then we will give you the strategies you need to avoid these mistakes and achieve your financial goals, whether your goals involve buying a house, a college education for your children, or a stress free retirement.

The problem is you have been screwed and may not even know it. You, along with your fellow middle-class Americans have been screwed by a combination of taxes, interest and a lack of critical information. We wrote "Unscrewed" to give you the knowledge you need to slash your tax bill and go from paying taxes forever ... to paying taxes never!

To teach you these strategies and secrets, we have worked diligently to keep this book simple. Of course, the financial community has worked very hard to keep you confused about your finances by using acronyms and a cryptic language understood by only the elites and the rich. We will provide you with the key to decipher those acronyms and that cryptic language.

Here is the bottom line: This book will show you the roadblocks you will face, while providing you with an easy road map to follow so that you can reach your destination of retirement success. Retirement success has many definitions, but for us, the cornerstone of retirement success must be ... **that you never out- live your money!**

INTRODUCTION

As you know, we are living in a time of great financial uncertainty and increasing government control of our lives and future.

We think you'll agree that the traditional methods of saving and investing for retirement have not worked well. Whether it was the stock market roller-coaster ride, your shrunken 401(k), IRA, or the low-interest rate you receive on your CD's or bank accounts, things have not gone as planned for you or the rest of the middle class.

Now to make things even worse, many experts predict you will be hit by **higher taxes** to pay for our exploding national debt and **out-of-control government spending**. Add all these things together and we have the makings of a real disaster for your retirement planning.

Many of the people we trusted in the past to guide our financial retirement success can no longer be depended upon. These include the stock brokers, fund managers, bankers, politicians, and talking heads on TV dishing out bad advice. While we are pointing fingers, let's not forget the vast majority of insurance brokers and agents collecting big commissions selling you financial products that may not be in your best interest. So what's the answer? What can you do to protect yourself and not outlive your retirement money?

In a nutshell ...you must take control of your own future!

Here are some strong comments from the late comedian George Carlin on the crux of the problem you are facing.

1

"They (the owners of this country) don't want a well-informed well-educated population capable of critical thinking ...They don't want that, it isn't in their best interest ... They don't want people who are smart enough to sit around the kitchen table and know about a system that threw them under the bus thirty years ago., They don't want that., They want obedient workers ... they want you to be smart enough to run their machines and do the paperwork but just dumb enough to passively accept all these increasingly sh$%ier jobs with lower pay, longer hours, reduced benefits and the end of overtime, the vanishing pension that goes away the minute you go to collect it, and now they're coming for your social security ... They're coming for your f@#!%&*g retirement!

They want it back so they can give it to their criminal friends on Wall Street. ...You know something? ... They will get it! Because they own this f@#&!n place. It is a big club and you ain't in it. You and I are not in the big club. ... By the way, it's the same club they beat you over the head with all day long telling you with their media, what to believe ... what to think ... and what to buy, ... The table is tilted folks ... The game is rigged and nobody seems to notice... Nobody seems to care."

Although you may find this a bit strong, Carlin told it like he saw it-- certainly a rarity today! Now, let's be honest with each other. Nobody is going to care more about you and your family than you. It's your money and if you don't learn to take control of your own future, there are no second chances regarding your retirement. You will live or die with your decisions.

Since there are no do-over's or second chances, it is more critical than ever for you to be well informed and make decisions that will protect your future. Those who refuse to educate themselves will work until they drop and will likely be solely dependent on family, friends and government hand-outs for their retirement.

That's the bad news, now the good news. In this book, you will learn the basics of retirement investments ... **and how to always protect your retirement savings from any losses**.

This is powerful stuff and the authors of this book will show you WHY self-education regarding your finances is the first step to retirement! We will teach you HOW to pay 0 percent income tax WHEN you retire.

We will also teach you WHO to choose--the right broker, agent or financial adviser to partner with you--so that you actually achieve your retirement goals. Most importantly we will help you learn WHAT you can do today to have a successful tomorrow!

CHAPTER 1: WHY SHOULD I CARE ABOUT RETIREMENT PLANNING?

When I was young I thought that money was the most important thing in life; now that I am old I know that it is.
— Oscar Wilde

You have a big problem! Or to state that more accurately, you and the rest of America's more than 300 million people have a big problem ... a very big problem!

As you already know, we are living in very turbulent and dangerous times. Read any newspaper or, magazine, watch any TV news program, or listen to any talk radio show and you instantly realize America is in deep trouble.

Politicians of both parties spend our children's and grand children's money like drunken sailors or crack addicts. They use our hard-earned tax money to bail out too-big-to-fail banks, credit card companies, and corporations with corporate welfare ... that you pay for. Then they drain your retirement safety net-called Social Security and Medicare ... like blood-thirsty vampires.

In order to keep this deck of cards they created from collapsing, what do they do? Why they print more and more Monopoly money to pay for their uncontrolled spending, of course. As you can imagine, the effect of printing paper money with nothing to back it will eventually lead to both inflation and the devaluation of your retirement funds.

Now add to this dismal picture, the high likelihood of your taxes skyrocketing to pay for all of this out-of-control government spending and you may very well find that your existing retirement plan is nearly worthless.

A number of factors have gotten us to where we are today. First, we have unscrupulous politicians pandering to human greed and class warfare as they steal money from your Social Security and Medicare. Then we have the Wall Street gangsters who have a special talent for duping Main Street investors.

The Wall Street gangsters pushed their concept of buying-and-holding stocks ahead of the worst decade long-performance in stocks since the Great Depression. This same gang and their partners in crime pushed the dot-com bubble, subprime mortgage crisis, and the concept of buying-and-flipping houses.

Then, as you may remember, they bailed out politically connected, too-big-to--fail companies and mega banks with your tax dollars. As a special thank you for the use of your tax dollars, these same mega banks refuse to give you a loan when you need it and then nickel and dime you to death ... if you ever dare to bounce a check.

Surely you have heard the promise many financial advisors make that once you retire your cost of living will be dramatically reduced. The reason they give for this is that after you retire and drop out of the rat race, you won't need as much money because you will down size your lifestyle and your needs.

Now, that sounds great except for a couple small issues. The first is the effect of **higher taxes** on everything you buy or use, including your fixed retirement income.

The second is the effect of the government's continued wild spending, borrowing from countries like China and printing money 24 hours a day. Clearly this will devalue your fixed retirement income and cause devastating inflation-requiring more dollars in retirement ... not less.

Well, now that we got that out of the way, it's time to identify some <u>additional challenges to your retirement funds</u> that are rarely mentioned by the media gurus or financial advisors. However, these challenges can also dramatically affect your retirement plan, so please pay attention so that you don't have to spend your retirement standing in front of Walmart greeting customers.

#1: Not All Health Care Costs Are Covered by Medicare:

Do not make the mistake of believing that you and your spouse will have all your health care costs covered by Medicare. What you will find is that you and your spouse could be billed for thousands of dollars in premiums, co-pays, coinsurance, or deductible payments for your medical and prescription plans as you age and your medical needs increase.

#2: Your Adult Children May Need Your Support:

With the economy in a shambles and job prospects poor, college graduates are moving back in with their parents in record numbers. Naturally, should this joyous event occur, you may have other related expenses, such as paying for their down payments for their homes, student loans, and weddings, etc.

#3: Your Parents May Need Your Support:

As people live longer, you may find yourself caring for or paying bills for an aging parent. This could be an additional strain on your retirement budget, especially if your parents did not have sufficient retirement savings themselves.

#4: You May Have to Hire People:

Before you retired there were many tasks you did without a second thought: planting a garden, mowing the lawn, trimming trees, house cleaning, car repairs, moving to a new home, unpacking, etc. Now you will be paying someone to do all this for you.

These are just a few of the challenges you may face in your retirement, and this is why this book can be such a critical guide to teach you the strategies needed to never outlive your retirement money.

Here is a quick warning and a caution: If you listen to the news media, the financial shows, or our government leaders, you will hear a constant drum beat telling you how we have turned the corner and things are improving daily. They will tell you unemployment is going down, the stock market and housing market are going up and happy days are here again. If you believe them, somebody will be selling you a bridge in Brooklyn shortly.

In spite of this, every once in a while the media controllers fail to censor the truth. Here is an excerpt of a straight forward on-line article written by Edward "Ted" Siedle for Forbes.com:

"We are on the precipice of the greatest retirement crisis in the history of the world. In the decades to come, we will witness millions of elderly Americans, the Baby Boomers and others, slipping into poverty. Too frail to work, too poor to retire will become the "new normal" for many elderly Americans.

That dire prediction, which I wrote two years ago, is already coming true. Our national demographics, coupled with indisputable glaringly insufficient retirement savings and human physiology, suggest that a catastrophic outcome for at least a significant percentage of our elderly population is inevitable. With the average 401(k) balance for 65 year olds estimated at $25,000 by independent experts – $100,000 if you believe the retirement planning industry - the decades many elders will spend in forced or elected "retirement" will be grim.

Corporate America and the financial wizards behind the past three decades of so-called retirement innovations, most notably titans of the pension benefits consulting and mutual fund 401(k) industries, are down-playing just how bad things are already and how much worse they are going to get.

Americans today are aware that corporate pensions have been virtually eliminated and that the few remaining private, as well as the nation's public pensions, are in jeopardy. Even if you are among the lucky few that have a pension, you cannot rest assured that it will be there for all the years you'll need it.

Whether you know it or not, someone is busy trying to figure how to screw you out of your pension. Americans also know that the great 401(k) experiment of the past 30 years has been a disaster. It is now apparent that 401(k) s will not provide the retirement security promised to workers."

This article comes from a financial expert, not an angry anti-establishment comedian like George Carlin. If you are in the shrinking American middle class you need to be afraid … very afraid!

We have one other **dirty little secret** to share with you to demonstrate how you and the rest of the middle class are being screwed. You probably won't be seeing this on your TV news or in your favorite newspaper. Here are some excerpts from a recent article by David Malpass that should get your attention.

"From 1999 through 2007 the real median household income fell 1 percent. It fell another 4 percent during the 2008-2009 recession. And then, incredibly, the real median income fell again during the recovery dropping an estimated 5 percent in 2010-2013."

"Although the U.S. Labor Department in July, of 2013 was reporting unemployment at over 7 percent, the real number is over 14 percent if you count workers who are underemployed or those who have given up searching for work" ... and this does not count the millions of American jobs that have been down-sized from full time to part time due to the new Affordable Care Act (Obamacare).

Here is the bottom line: Your money is being redistributed by corrupt politicians and the Federal Reserve Banking System (non-government entity) to make the rich richer and you and your family more dependent on the government ... and much easier to control.

The Federal Reserve has become the biggest transfer program to the rich, channeling cheap credit to the government and big business and it comes at the expense of small businesses ... and you!

Keeping long term interest rates low is a gift to the rich who do most of the long-term borrowing using their high incomes and valuable assets as collateral. The burden falls on your retirement funds and savings accounts as you receive virtually no interest on your CD's, annuities, etc. as the rich get richer and you get poorer.

This is one of the reasons this book can be so critical to you and your retirement as we will teach you the techniques you will need to survive and prosper in spite of the game being rigged against you!

"OUR RETIREMENT PROGRAM IS THAT YOU CAN RESIGN WHENEVER YOU WANT TO."

SUMMARY

- Increasing taxes, inflation and unexpected costs can be devastating to your retirement plan.

- It's your money, and you get only one chance to get it right. There are no do-over's or second chances!

- No one will ever care as much about you and your family as you do. That is why you need new strategies so that you never outlive your retirement money.

- Remember those that fail to plan …will fail!

CHAPTER 2: THE BIGGEST RETIREMENT MISTAKES ARE?

"The question isn't at what age I want to retire, it's at what income."

— *George Foreman*

It seems that our government and politicians have a lot in common with Count Dracula. Both suck the life out of their victims. One removes all your blood and the other removes as much of your money as they can get away with ... in the form of taxes.

One of the tactics used by our government, politicians, bankers, and Wall Street to confuse you and the rest of the middle class is their use of a strange, made-up financial language. It is a confusing alphabet soup of terminology and language such as 401(k), IRA, qualified plan, non-qualified plan, etc. If you are not familiar with any of this made-up language, you're at a distinct disadvantage.

It would be like moving to France and never learning to speak French, but expecting to be successful living there. Makes sense, right? So before we get into the specific investments, let's work together to get you a little more fluent in the language of money ... your retirement money.

There are two common terms you will hear and read in any financial discussion regarding retirement. These two terms are "qualified" and "non-qualified" plans.

What Is a Qualified Plan?

A **qualified plan** is designed to offer you tax benefits in addition to your regular retirement plans, such as IRA's. While you are still working, employers deduct an allowable portion of pretax wages from your paycheck, and the contributions and your earnings then grow tax-deferred until withdrawal. Typical qualified plans are:

- 401(k) (457 and 403B are similar)
- IRA (except for the Roth IRA)
- SEP
- MSA

What Is a Non-Qualified Plan?

A **non-qualified plan** is not eligible for tax-deferral benefits. Because of this fact, any of your deducted contributions for non-qualified plans are taxed like your regular income. Typical non-qualified plans are:

- CD's
- Stocks
- Mutual Funds
- Bonds
- Annuities (unless they are in an IRA)
- Life Insurance

Qualified Plans Versus Non-Qualified Plans:

The basic difference between these two terms is related to how your money is treated by the IRS for taxing purposes. Although it sounds better to be qualified as opposed to non-qualified, believe it or not, there can be significant advantages for your savings to be non-qualified vehicles. You will see this later in the book.

First, let's focus on some qualified plans. Remember a qualified plan refers to an IRS tax code provision, and these are all tax deductible and tax deferred with the exception of a Roth IRA. These qualified plans grow tax deferred, with a choice of investments such as mutual funds, stocks, bonds, etc. Simply put, a qualified investment is one where the taxes on your invested dollars and interest earned have **NOT** been paid yet.

<u>Examples of Qualified Plans:</u>

The 401(k) is, without any doubt, the granddaddy of all qualified retirement vehicles. Unfortunately for most Americans, this is the beginning-and sadly the end-of their savings strategy.

"401(k)" refers to the tax code and is a provision, in the tax code for employees that allows you to have tax-deductible and tax-deferred savings. If you are lucky your employer can match a certain percentage of your contribution … which is a very good thing.

A 457 plan is a similar provision in the tax code for government employees while the 403(b) plan is for employees of non-profits such as colleges, schools and charities. These operate in a similar manner as the 401(k).

An IRA (Individual Retirement Account) can be used in addition to the other qualified plans providing another place to put money in your choice of investments that are also tax deductible and tax deferred.

Note: Although the Roth IRA is similar to the traditional IRA, your money deposited is not tax deductible; however, unlike the other IRA's your money can be withdrawn **tax free.**

SEP: (Simplified Employment Pension Plan):

This is a provision in the tax code for a small-business person or sole proprietor and is similar to a 401(k) but without any percentage matching.

MSA: (Medical Savings Account):

This is another provision in the tax code that allows you to put money away for medical expenses. It is similar to the IRA, but it allows tax-free withdrawals **for medical expenses only.**

Investment vehicles: Can either be qualified or nonqualified ... **and can be subject to risk of loss of your principal or investment.**

Examples of Non-qualified Plans:

CD's: (Certificate of Deposit):

We prefer to call them "Certificates of Depreciation." They are generally offered by banks or credit unions. The monies are insured up to $250,000 by the FDIC (Federal Deposit Insurance Corporation). The CD's require you to maintain your monies in the account for a contractual period-generally six months to five years-in return for a guaranteed interest rate that is usually very low. Early withdrawal will trigger financial penalties.

Stocks:

This is a type of security that gives you some ownership in a corporation and gives you a claim for a portion of the corporation's assets and earnings.

Mutual Funds:

Mutual funds are several stocks bundled together and usually chosen by professional fund managers. They are designed to outperform the S&P (Standard and Poor) composite of the 500 largest companies publicly traded.

Bonds:

This is a debt investment in which you loan money to an entity (corporate or governmental) for a set period of time at a set interest rate. These bonds are commonly used by companies and governments (foreign, U.S. federal, state and local) to pay for various projects and activities.

Annuities:

An annuity is a contract between you and an insurance company to invest money with that company. Your investment can either be in a lump sum or in a series of payments. In return for your investment you can receive a regular payment (generally with interest) beginning immediately or at some point in the future.

Life insurance:

This is a protection against loss of income that would result if the person insured were to pass away during the life of an insurance contract. Upon the death of the insured, the beneficiary listed would receive the proceeds of the insurance policy thereby safeguarding the beneficiary from the financial impact of the death of the person insured.

Now that we have provided you a basic understanding and some fluency in the language of money, it's time to move on to the biggest retirement mistakes many people make.

Mistake #1: The first and single biggest mistake people make is not taking the time to educate themselves regarding their own finances:

The reason self-education is necessary is there are too many conflicting and confusing theories about handling your finances. However, we are not suggesting that you need to know every term to understand the basic principles related to a successful retirement plan.

Mistake #2: Not paying yourself first:

A book by George Samuel Clason called The Richest Man in Babylon written in 1926 said it best: *"A part of all you earn is yours to keep."*

Mistake #3: The failure to understand how much taxation, interest and inflation will affect your future financial plans:

We have gone to great lengths to gather substantive, credible and verifiable information that will help you understand that most of your financial gains going forward will come from tax avoidance.

Louis D. Brandeis was a famous United States Supreme Court Justice from 1919 to 1939. The following are some of his fascinating thoughts on tax avoidance:

"I lived in Alexandria, Virginia. Near the Supreme Court chambers is a toll bridge across the Potomac. When in a rush, I pay the toll and get home early. However, I usually drive outside the downtown section of the city and cross the Potomac on a free bridge. The bridge was placed outside the downtown Washington, D.C. area to serve a useful social service: getting drivers to drive an extra mile to help alleviate congestion during rush hour.

If I went over the toll bridge and through the barrier without paying the toll, I would be committing tax evasion. However, if I drive the extra mile outside the city of Washington and take the free bridge, I am using a legitimate, logical and suitable method of tax avoidance, and I am performing a useful social service by doing so."

"For my tax evasion, I should be punished. For my tax avoidance, I should be commended. The tragedy in life is that so few people know that the free bridge even exists."

Mistake #4: Commingling your savings and investments:

Many Americans frequently do this during difficult economic times and this is one of the primary reasons they don't have sufficient funds at retirement age ... a time when they need these funds the most.

Again, it makes no sense to put your savings in an inaccessible place, like a qualified plan, where you can't use your money ... just when you need it most.

Mistake #5: Not seeking professional assistance:

You should never risk your future retirement by trying to do it all yourself or on the Internet anymore than you would do your own dental work, or your own surgical procedures. Doing it yourself is probably more effective for maintaining your home or car than your retirement.

Mistake #6: Not taking advantage of the POWER of compound interest, tax deferral and tax free distributions:

This rule alone is the most important to understand and apply. *Albert Einstein once said "Compounding is mankind's greatest invention because it allows for the reliable, systematic accumulation of wealth."*

Mistake #7: Using inflexible plans such as IRA's and 401(k)'s as your primary savings and retirement plan:

Plans that penalize you for the use of your own money come to mind. Those plans that do not anticipate the unexpected are the most dangerous. Remember, the best laid plans of mice and men often go astray.

Reasons for Retiring Earlier or Later than Expected

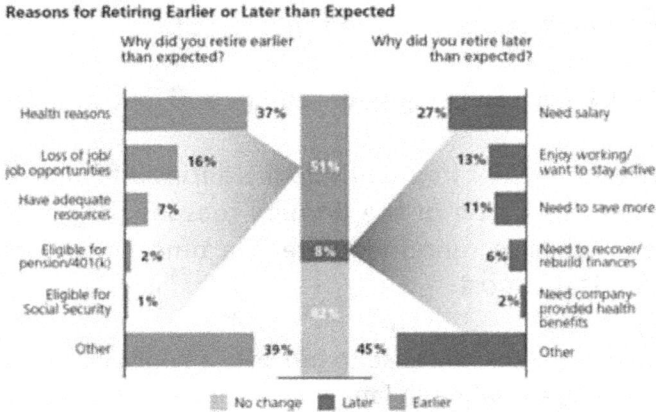

Source: MetLife Mature Market Institute, *Transitioning into Retirement*, Figure 1, 2012.

SUMMARY

- The granddaddy and most popular type of qualified plan is a 401(k).

- The most popular types of non-qualified plans are CD's and annuities.

- Investment vehicles can either be qualified or non-qualified and can be subject to risk of loss of your principal or investment.

- Lack of education will tax you the greatest.

- Pay yourself first.

- Don't underestimate your true taxation.

- Don't comingle savings and investments.

- Seek professional assistance.

- Use the power of compound interest.

- Create a flexible plan for multiple contingencies.

CHAPTER 3: THE COST OF NOT HAVING ACCESS TO YOUR MONEY

"Too many people spend money they earned, to buy things they don't want, to impress people that they don't like."
— *Will Rogers*

This is the crux of many of our money and retirement problems and it is really very important that we demonstrate how the financial deck has been stacked against you by the politicians in office. Once you understand the real situation, we will teach you some concepts so that you can win the game.

The first challenge you want to understand is that a major cause behind your lack of money now and in retirement is the true cost of taxes and interest. Let's start with taxes.

The problem with taxes goes far beyond the federal, state, and local income taxes we discussed earlier. If you are reading this and happen to be employed you know you have to pay a combined 7.85 percent for Medicare and Social Security taxes ... IN ADDITION to your federal, state and local taxes (~15.2 percent if self-employed).

You also are required to pay a multitude of other taxes and fees for virtually every aspect of your life, in addition to all the other taxes we mentioned. Oh, and one of the newest tax gifts you will be receiving from your friendly government representatives at the IRS and your thoughtful politicians comes from The Affordable Care Act (Obamacare).

If you think that's the end of it, here are some additional tax and fee booby traps you may have forgotten about: property, sales, mortgage, cable, telephone, cell phone, loan, automobile, license, credit card, bank account, gasoline, healthcare, travel, training, books, clothing, estate, inflation losses, inheritance, deficit allowance, gift, and, of course, capital gains-and too many others to mention.

In order to ensure you understand completely how this double taxation affects you and your money, let's use gasoline taxes as an example.

If you receive $100 of income and pay 30 percent in federal income tax, you are left with $70. Now you take your $70 and fill up your car with gasoline. Unfortunately, of the $70 needed to fill up your tank, 50 percent (or $35) is for fuel taxes.

So now the $64,000 question is: How much tax did you actually pay on your $100 of income in this scenario? The answer is 65 percent. Of the $100 you earned, $30 went to federal income tax, $35 went to fuel tax, and the remaining $35 went to the cost of gasoline. The takeaway for you is that you are being robbed and mugged by hidden taxes well beyond your federal, state and local taxes. This is truly a case of taxation without representation.

Although this is only the tip of the iceberg, you're probably starting to get the big picture here ... as we pull open the Wizard of Oz's curtain.

Let's look at an example of the actual tax rate you would have if your total annual family income is $85,000. If you looked at the Internal Revenue Service (IRS) federal income tax chart, you might believe you're in the 28 percent tax bracket.

Barry Harrin and Raymond Leeper

Would you be shocked to learn that instead of the advertised federal income tax rate of 28 percent, you are actually paying an absolute minimum tax rate of 59.7 percent-or more-when you take into account all the taxes and fees previously discussed and estimated as of 2013? Essentially, if your income is $100,000 you actually get only $40,300 to live on. That doesn't seem like a fair deal for you or the rest of America!

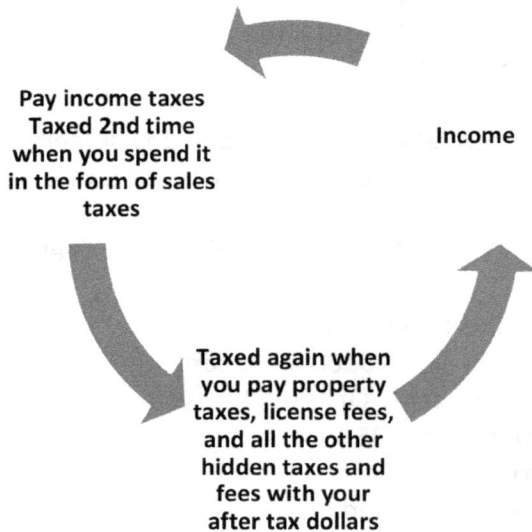

Pay income taxes
Taxed 2nd time
when you spend it
in the form of sales
taxes

Income

Taxed again when
you pay property
taxes, license fees,
and all the other
hidden taxes and
fees with your
after tax dollars

Now what really makes this even worse is that virtually anything you have to pay taxes or fees on has already been taxed before. Can you say double taxation? Think about it: virtually every penny you spend, whether you received it from your 401(k), IRA, salary, bank account, or Social Security has already been taxed before. Nice, right?

Oh, and don't forget to thank the politicians who generously redistributed your money to those they believed deserved it more than you did. If this hasn't raised your blood pressure ... then read on!

THE POWER CURVE

The power curve is an important concept that is directly related to the cost of not having money. The power curve can work *against* you with exponential force; conversely those same forces that work against you-can also work *for* you exponentially.

The power curve is an important concept you need to understand. It could be one of the keys to your future retirement success. The term "power curve" comes from the world of aviation and flying.

Simply put in aviation terms, this is the point when your plane has slowed down and in order to maintain your altitude, you have to start adding power again. Your engine is working as hard as it can, and you are burning your fuel like crazy, and you're still flying at your slowest speed possible. At this point, where you are barely hanging in the air, even a tiny cut back in your power will have your plane crashing to earth. At this point you are behind the power curve-not a good place to be in an airplane or in life.

"What does this have to do with my retirement?" You might be asking.

When Ray and Dale Leeper were 18 and 16, their dad Paul Leeper, sat them down and gave them a lesson they would never forget, one that will help you and your family be success-ful as well.

Consider your available money as your fuel for your family's financial airplane and your debt, taxes and interest as the drag or friction. To keep your financial airplane always flying high you must maximize your fuel (money) by reducing the drag (debt, taxes, and interest) on your airplane.

The following are the simple rules from the Leeper brothers on always keeping ahead of the power curve and keeping your family flying high:

- Pay yourself first
- Avoid interest
- Avoid taxes
- Aim high

According to the U.S. Census Bureau, "household median income" is defined as "the amount which divides the income distribution into two equal groups, half having income above that amount, and half having income below that amount."

The U.S. Census Bureau currently publishes median house-hold income data from 1967 until present day.

Year	No. of Households	Nominal $	Inflation Adjusted $
2011	121,084,000	$48,152	$50,054
1992	96,426,000	$28,870	$48,117

The median household income between 1992 and today has increased only ~4 percent (over 19 years 1992-2011), but the cost of gas per gallon has gone up 350 percent.

1992	VS.	2008
PRICE OF A GALLON OF REGULAR GASOLINE		
JULY 27, 1992		JULY 28, 2008
$1.13		**$3.96**

Data: Energy Information Administration

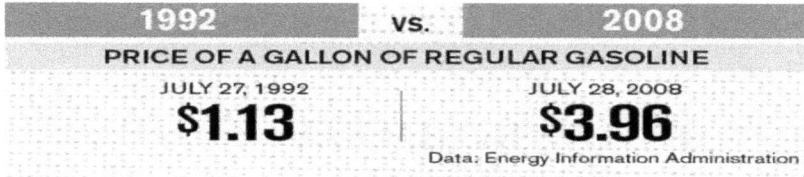

If we factor in inflation at ~3 percent per year, over 19 years that is a whopping 57 percent. So the average American income has actually decreased 53 percent (4 percent increase-57 percent inflation) over the past 19 years.

If you have been feeling like you have less money to spend now than in the past ... now you know why. Welcome to the shrinking American middle class!

SUMMARY

- Your real tax rate is much higher than your federal tax rate.

- You and the rest of your fellow Americans are being picked clean by your government and corrupt politicians through hidden fees and taxes.

- The power curve can either keep your retirement flying high or bring it crashing to the ground ... forcing you to wait in line for your government handouts.

- Nothing is more important to your financial future and your retirement savings than reducing your taxes and interest whenever possible.

CHAPTER 4: WHY FINDING THE RIGHT AGENT IS CRITICAL TO YOU

"I have never made a bad decision, but sometimes I get new information that makes my old decisions not seem so good."
— *Paul Leeper*

We have already determined that the decisions you make regarding your retirement are some of the most important decisions you'll ever make-and there are no do-over's.

Clearly the decisions you make regarding your financial retirement are only as good as the information you are basing your decisions on! So a good question to start with is: are you receiving the majority of your advice from someone who is on the securities (Wall Street) side of the market or from someone on the protection (insurance) side of the market?

The security side of the market refers to the Wall Street side where stocks, bonds, and mutual funds prevail. Interestingly enough, although they are called securities, you have already discovered ... stocks, bonds, and mutual funds can be anything but secure.

The bottom line here is that although the Wall Street or securities side of the market can offer you much higher returns **... all or part of your money is always at risk of loss!**

If you have a financial advisor who is on the securities side, often times their solutions and recommendations will involve securities. Generally, they are not as familiar with the protection side of the business which is why many investment advisors can't help you with cash-value life insurance or related long term care riders and tax-free aspects of these savings vehicles.

These advisors understand the stock market and can guide you to which mutual funds you should buy. They preach long-term growth in the market. They coined the phrase "buy and hold for the long term."

Now don't get us wrong here, you do need to put your money into action by taking advantage of any tax benefits your government allows or matching funds your company offers as part of your overall retirement plan.

However, too many American's use their 401(k) or similar vehicle as not only their investment option, but also as their primary-and possibly their only-savings vehicle ... which is a major mistake!

Now let's look at the other side of the market, the protection or insurance side. The late Paul Leeper, founder of the Leeper Insurance Group got into the insurance or protection side of the market over 30 years ago.

Paul was a great teacher and began training his sons Dale and Ray when they were teenagers and continued to train them for over 25 years on how to protect their client's money and their financial retirement. His favorite tag line to the boys was: *"If people really understood how good this stuff was, they would be lined up at the door to buy it!"*

Dale and Ray now run the agency, and after many years of their dad's training and experience, they have developed unique protection strategies and a vast array of products with the highest-rated insurance companies. This is a combination that is not easily duplicated, which is why this chapter is very important to your retirement success.

Here is what you are up against. It is common knowledge in the insurance industry that over the past 5 to 10 years both the physical number of agents and their level of training have dropped significantly.

The number of licensed agents dwindles every day. Many life and health agents have left the business as an unintended consequence of our healthcare reform, increasing government control, and the complexity of some of the newer life insurance and annuity products

Many of the remaining agents tend to focus on simpler products, such as term life, mortgage, and burial insurance. As experienced old-timers leave the business, fewer new agents enter the business.

Here is your challenge. Tougher economic times require you to find that elusive top 10 percent of what we call great agents. These are the few agents that have the knowledge, the contracts with the top-rated companies and the integrity to put your best interests ahead of their own desires for big commissions.

Great agents can be found in every state, but there are no bill boards on the highway to help you differentiate a great agent from a mediocre agent. There are many variables in any plan, but a great agent takes those variables into account and designs a plan that is in harmony with your desires, needs and objectives.

Great life insurance agents should understand your tax situation, your intermediate and long term goals as well as your budget. They will offer the very best products because they understand they will get only one chance to prove their strategy to you.

These agents know the products they sell and the products they don't sell, whether they are products in the protection industry (e.g., like life insurance, long-term care) or financial products in the securities industry, such as mutual funds and bonds.

Great agents also understand that investments and savings do not go into the same bucket. These agents never risk your money to loss; they design a plan based on your objectives, whether it be cash value or death benefit.

As an example, if a client has a goal to have X amount of money distributed to him/her tax free at some specified point in the future, then the agent should design a plan with the least amount of death benefit possible, so that a majority of the funds paid into the plan goes towards increasing his/her cash savings and meeting that client's financial objectives.

Unfortunately, agents are primarily paid for the insurance they sell and have the flexibility to adjust the death benefit in any proposal; this allows them to immediately increase their take or commission … and the average consumer will never know the difference.

If you bought the same policy from the same company with everything else being equal, then the agent and his or her greed factor becomes your greatest variable. Most importantly, your agent needs to be on board with your goals and objectives … not their own sales goals and objectives.

A great agent will also follow up every year after the plan is implemented to make sure your plan stays on track and to help to outline options and make adjustments if necessary!

There are bad apples in every industry, including the life insurance industry, and one might say "there are a lot of bears in the woods" to watch out for. Much of the negative perception of our industry comes from the agents who know nothing more about the product than how their commissions are derived ... and sometimes not even that much.

They do not show you how you can take money out, only how to put it in. They will unknowingly (or knowingly) sell you products that are-just simply put-inappropriate. Some know better; some don't. Either way, it ends up giving the industry a black eye.

The run-of-the-mill agent may ask a few questions, listen to you a little, and then offer you a $250,000, $500,000, or higher term life policy or a really big commission 1950's-type whole life insurance policy if they are really trying to make the payments on their Mercedes.

Another give away that will help you determine if you are dealing with a not-so-great agent is if he or she seems aggressive right after he or she finds out what monthly premium you can afford to pay.

The great agent, on the other hand, will go through a lot of intense fact finding questions with you. These will include your current financial and family situation as well as future plans for your children, such as college and, wedding expenses, in addition to your retirement plans and objectives.

Depending on how complex your situation is, the great agent may not even want to discuss any products or options with you at your first meeting. They may choose instead to review everything you have told them back at their office. This agent won't be aggressive or try to close a sale quickly as he or she is more interested in doing what's right for you rather than for him or her.

Before they set up a second appointment, they will most likely run many examples with different products until they find the best two or three that fit your specific situation only ... because that great agent knows that one size does not fit all!

These are some of the things you will want to watch for ... in choosing your great agent!

SUMMARY

- Learn the difference between the investment (Wall Street) side and protection (insurance) side of the business regarding your retirement plans.

- Pay a lot of attention to the following actions your current or prospective agent makes. If you observe any of these indications it may be time to keep looking for that great agent:

  - Agent is aggressive and ready to get you to sign an application.

  - Agent does not do a comprehensive fact finder or, at a minimum, ask a lot of detailed questions regarding:

    - Your family and financial situation.

    - Your retirement goals and objectives.

CHAPTER 5: WHAT IS LIFE INSURANCE?

"You need life insurance if somebody will suffer financially when you die"

— David Woods

What is the history of life insurance?

The concept of life insurance is very old and in fact it has been around in one form or other since the time of the Roman Empire. It began in ancient Rome as a way to cover funeral costs of members of burial clubs.

After the death of a club member, the leftover monies would be distributed to the departed's surviving family members to prevent impoverishment. It sounds pretty similar to our basic life insurance in modern times, although there have been many twists and turns along the way.

In Europe during the Middle Ages, a support system similar to the Roman burial clubs developed. As the European society became more urbanized, groups of craftsman formed guilds, which would be similar to today's union shops.

These guilds, especially in the larger cities developed formalized procedures that would provide financial support to the families of guild members when they died.

By the end of the 1600's, the first mortality table was developed, attempting to predict an individual's lifespan, which was one of the first attempts to calculate premiums. Interestingly this table was developed by the discoverer of Halley's Comet, one Edmond Halley.

One of the first examples of life insurance in the New World began in the United States before the Revolutionary War. Churches such as the Presbyterian and Episcopalian organized funding for widows and orphans as well as their priests. A few of these developed into companies that some consider the beginning of what is now our life insurance industry.

Although there were a number of life insurance companies, such as Mass Mutual and New York Life, during the time of the American Civil War, it would take another century before the life insurance industry really took off.

The defining moment that turned the ultra conservative life insurance industry on its head came in 1977 when Arthur L. "Art" Williams Jr. founded the A.L. Williams Company later known as Primerica Financial Services.

Up until this point the major product in the life insurance industry had been expensive, cash-value whole life or permanent insurance. However, Williams' marketing brilliance and unforgettable slogan of "Buy term and invest the difference" forever changed the industry.

William's convinced many customers to switch from their conventional whole life insurance policies to the much less expensive term life insurance. His company rapidly grew and became the largest seller of life insurance in the United States.

As you'll see shortly, William's slogan of "Buy term and invest the difference" has been borrowed by some of our media financial guru's and unfortunately ... not always in your best interest!

Today, the U.S. life insurance industry is one of the most powerful and stable parts of the American financial system. It has over $5 trillion in assets and approximately $20 trillion in estimated coverage, and the inventory of outstanding policies to consumers numbers in the hundreds of millions.

What is life insurance?

Life insurance is a contract that pays your beneficiaries a death benefit for a payment of a premium. The amount of the benefit should take into account your needs while you are alive and your family's needs when you pass on. A person must be relatively healthy to purchase a life insurance policy.

Types of life insurance include term, cash value whole life, universal life, indexed universal life and variable life insurance. Rates are based on risk to the company related to your age, health, tobacco use and driving history. The type of policy and potential length of contract also play into the rates or premiums.

The policies that have the lowest cost to the consumer are the policies that have the smallest claims potential to the insurance company. The death benefit associated with life insurance transfers to the designated beneficiaries outside probate court and without taxation.

Why do you need life insurance?

In today's difficult economic times, many Americans struggle simply to pay their day to day expenses. The death of a bread winner can be a devastating financial blow to the surviving spouse and children, bringing great pain and suffering to those you love.

In spite of this, **approximately 95 million adult Americans are without life insurance**, according to LIMRA, an insurance industry research group. "The fact is, the vast majority of

Americans need life insurance and, sadly, most people either have none or not enough."

Although it seems obvious that you will never be as young as you are now-this is especially important when it comes to life insurance. It makes good financial sense to get coverage when you are young and healthy, because your premiums are based on your age and health. Generally, for most cash value policies your premiums are locked in over the life of the policy … **and can't be increased due to any change in your health status.**

One day life is going along smoothly, and the next you're thrown a curve ball. No one knows what the future holds. None of us expect to die prematurely, but the truth is … **roughly 600,000 people die each year in the prime of their lives.**

That is why today is always the best day to protect your family and take care of your life insurance needs. Besides that, no one (aside from your agent) is going to pat you on the back and tell you what a responsible and loving thing you are doing for your family by purchasing life insurance.

It seems there are a lot more dads' today that would rather spend their money on cars, boats and motorcycles than protecting their family should the unthinkable happen. Unlike when you buy a new car, boat, or motorcycle, no one is going to come up to you and say, "Wow! That sure is a nice policy you got there!" That will never happen. But what will happen?

You will die, bills will need to be paid and the IRS will want their tax money … these things are unavoidable. Assuming you did the right thing before you die, somebody you loved very much is going to pull out this policy from your important papers. When they open this policy, it will speak volumes about you … and most of all, volumes about what you thought about them!

What are the major types of life insurance available?

Term Life Insurance:

The first type of life insurance is called "term life." Consider this like renting a house for a set period of time, but it is not an asset, nor does it have any cash value. However, this can be a very important and useful product depending upon your situation.

This kind of policy is established for a specific number of years before it expires. The most common term life policies cover 10 to 15 years, but life insurance companies have begun offering longer terms up to 30 years.

A term life insurance policy is usually a lot less expensive than cash value whole life insurance, because it covers you for only a set number of years and the commission to the agent is generally lower.

Although term policies tend to be less expensive, there are some downsides: because there is no cash value on these type of policies, you cannot take out a loan. When your term of 10, 15, 20, or more years ends, your rates will be considerably higher ... **that is if you can even qualify medically for a new policy at that point in your life.**

Essentially, term insurance is a temporary form of life insurance and a big money maker for the insurance companies. Why, you ask? The answer is really quite simple. **Historically, term life policies have paid the death benefit to only 2 percent of the policy holders (according to LIMRA Facts).** Now you can understand why the insurance companies really love term insurance.

Whole Life or Cash Value Insurance:

The other type of life insurance available is whole life insurance also known as cash value insurance. In general, a whole life policy is permanent insurance that combines both life coverage and a savings fund. The policy pays a set, fixed amount on your death, and part of your premium goes toward building cash value from investments made by the insurance company.

Your cash value will build tax-deferred each year that you keep the policy in force. You are able to borrow against the cash fund that you accumulated without being taxed. The amount of premium you pay usually doesn't change throughout the life of the policy.

There are a number of different versions of cash value life insurance. Consider this similar to purchasing an asset you own, such as a house that would increase in value each year. This type of policy provides coverage until you die, assuming you continue paying your premiums.

Whole life policies are generally far more expensive than other options, and provide the agent with a higher commission. Although whole life policies are more expensive than term life, there are some advantages: whole life policies generally last until the death of the insured, and your premiums do not increase.

These policies build cash value and you have the option to take out low-or no-interest and tax-free loans (depending on your policy). The traditional or plain-Jane cash value whole life insurance policies have not changed dramatically over the years.

Universal Life Insurance Basics

As a form of permanent life protection, universal life insurance has three main characteristics. The first is a death benefit that remains in force for the balance of your life and transfers to your beneficiaries upon your death. The second is a cash value that grows steadily over time as you continue to pay premiums. The third is that a universal life policy offers flexible premiums.

Flexible premiums allow you to increase premiums in good times and reduce or stop premiums in bad times. In addition, the cash value of your policy can be tapped using either a tax free loan or a permanent cash withdrawal.

What are your returns?

Universal life insurance policies can be both safer and more convenient than many other long-term investment vehicles. Regardless of the state of the economy, universal life policies can produce average annual returns of between 2 to 6 percent as of this writing.

Insurance companies offering universal life insurance use a variety of techniques to achieve these gains. A number of them will use your premiums to purchase baskets of long-term bank-backed securities, such as CDs and money market funds. Others may link your policy to exchange-traded products, such as stocks, bonds, or mutual funds using a technique known as equity indexing.

Universal life insurance was one of the few financial vehicles that consistently delivered positive returns each year, even during the recent financial crisis. This is probably a result of universal life investments being more diversified than an average investment account; therefore it can be less risky during turbulent financial times.

Compared to a tax-deferred IRA, that requires you to either pay taxes when you make a deposit or a withdrawal, a universal life insurance policy can save your beneficiaries thousands of dollars in tax costs.

Additional Benefits:

One of the problems with IRA's is that your annual contributions are limited to a fairly low level. Unlike the IRA the growth of your cash value universal life policy is limited only by the size of the premium you want to pay and your death benefit. The total amount of your tax savings will increase in proportion to the size of your policy's face value.

Your universal life policy, unlike traditional retirement vehicles (401(k)'s and IRA's), is not subject to limits on temporary loans or penalties for early cash withdrawals. Life insurance cash values also don't impose a 10 percent penalty on withdrawals you make when you are under the age of 59 ½ years of age. You can access your cash value in a policy penalty-free loan, at any time, and for any reason.

The bottom line is that unlike your 401(k) or IRA, a universal or whole life policy allows you and your beneficiaries' almost unlimited access to your cash on a tax-free basis and could provide an important safety net in case of death or a chronic illness.

Remember, inside your universal life policy your money is tax-deferred, and you can take money out as a tax-free loan. You pay tax only on the earnings if you were to withdraw money from the policy. Also the death benefit passes tax-free to your heirs, which is why these policies are a great way to transfer wealth and, avoid probate court and for inheritance planning.

In addition, your policy can be protected from creditors in case of bankruptcy or judgments against you if you lose a lawsuit- and your life insurance policy can't be taken from you in these cases.

Also, lump sum or single premium life insurance (SPL) policies are also creditor protected, which means that in the event of some financial problem such as bankruptcy or other creditor seizure, your life policy can't be attached or taken from you to satisfy the claims of your creditors.

On a Side Note:

What you don't know can hurt you! According to a survey done by the Guardian Insurance Company and Life, a startling 60 percent of those interviewed between the ages of 20-30 do not know the difference between term life insurance and permanent life insurance.

Of those surveyed in this age group, 30 percent did not know what type of life insurance they owned and 19 percent did not know how much it would pay out. Nearly 20 percent said they did not need to get their own insurance, because their spouse was covered at work. If they only knew the truth! This proves that there is a very big disconnect between the young consumer and the insurance industry.

How Life Insurance Saved Well Known Companies:

Disneyland:

Walt Disney (1901-1966) and his brother Roy founded the Walt Disney Studio in 1923 in Los Angeles. In 1928, the studio debuted the now world famous character Mickey Mouse in the first cartoon with synchronized sound. It was an instant hit.

The Walt Disney Studio built on this great success with animated features and then television programs into the 1950's. This is when Walt's genius and ability to create magic for kids and their families led him to the idea of creating a unique amusement park that both children and their parents could enjoy together.

This was certainly a radical concept in the 1950's when the vast majority of amusement parks were rundown places filled with rough-looking people. Disney's vision was an amusement park that was family oriented, spotlessly clean, and filled with innovative attractions.

Unfortunately, the bankers and lenders of Disney's time failed to buy into his vision, and he was denied the funding he needed. Incredibly, Disney decided to become his own banker by borrowing money on his home and from his personal cash value insurance policies. When **Disneyland** opened in 1955, it became an instant success ... and the rest is history.

J.C. Penney:

James Cash Penney (1875-1971) got his start as an entrepreneur in 1898 when he was just an employee in a Golden Rule Store which was part of a small chain of dry goods stores. He was such an industrious worker that the owners of the chain offered him a one-third partnership in a new store they were opening in Kemmerer, Wyoming.

Penney did so well that the owners allowed him to participate in two other stores. When the original partners decided to dissolve their partnership in 1907, Penney took the opportunity to purchase complete ownership in his three stores.

Penney seemed to have a real knack for the business and by 1912 he was operating 34 stores throughout the Rocky Mountain region. Seizing upon his obvious success, he moved his company headquarters to Salt Lake City in 1913 and incorporated under the name you will still recognize as the J.C. Penney Company.

Penney was riding high as he expanded his empire to 1400 stores by 1929. Unfortunately, the stock market crash of 1929 and the devastating Great Depression brought Penney to his knees as his store sales and personal wealth rapidly disappeared.

The financial calamity and stress it caused affected both his health and mental state. He was having great difficulty in coming up with enough money to pay his workers and keep his stores open. Like many other business people during the Great

Depression, getting bank loans or lines of credit was a virtual impossibility.

Luckily for Penney and his thousands of employees, he was able to borrow against his cash value life insurance policies and paid his employees and the expenses of the day-to-day operations. Today, the company's operates over 1,100 stores in 50 states and takes in revenues of over $17 billion a year.

McDonald's:

The story began in 1954 when Ray Kroc (1902-1984) was working as a distributer of milkshake machines. Ray, always the entrepreneur, was trying to sell some of his milkshake machines to brothers Dick and Mac McDonald who owned a busy hamburger joint in San Bernardino, California.

After several discussions with the McDonald brothers, Kroc, 52 partnered with them as their nationwide franchising agent. He opened his first McDonald's restaurant in Des Plaines, Illinois, in 1955 and ultimately bought out the McDonald brothers in 1961.

Like many entrepreneurs, Kroc decided not to take a salary for a number of years as there were constant cash-flow difficulties. Like most small businesses in the early years, cash is king and without it the business can shrivel up and die.

The bankers, never known for their generosity or risk tolerance were very reluctant to give Kroc all the money he requested for his upstart hamburger joint-especially one that wanted the money to start an advertising campaign based on some crazy-looking clown named Ronald McDonald.

In a desperate search for advertising money, Kroc borrowed the balance of the needed funds from his cash value life insurance policy ... and the rest is history. Today, McDonald's serves more than 50 million people each day at over 34,000 locations worldwide with revenues of more than $27 billion.

If not for cash value life insurance, Disneyland might have been just a figment of Walt Disney's imagination; the J.C. Penney chain a casualty of the Great Depression, and McDonald's restaurants might have been nothing more than a few hamburger joints.

So the bottom line here is that the ability to fund yourself and your family in times of need or financial distress can be a real life saver. Having access to a cash value life insurance emergency fund can save you in desperate times, much as it did for Walt Disney, James Cash Penney and Ray Kroc.

SUMMARY

- **Life insurance is not a new concept.**

- **Approximately 95 million adult Americans are without life insurance.**

- **Roughly 600,000 people die each year in the prime of their lives.**

- **Although term insurance is not right for everyone, there are situations where it is a good solution.**

- **Universal life insurance can be an outstanding retirement vehicle when structured properly.**

- **Companies such as Disney, J.C. Penney, and McDonald's might not exist if it wasn't for cash value life insurance.**

CHAPTER 6: WHY MEDIA FINANCIAL GURU'S HATE LIFE INSURANCE?

"It is much easier to be critical than to be correct. "
--Benjamin Disraeli (1804-1881)

We are sure you have seen some of these financial gurus on TV or heard them on the radio. The first thing we need to do is differentiate between two types.

The first type would be the strictly stock-market gurus, such as Jim Cramer, and the other would be the financial wealth-management gurus, such as Dave Ramsey and Suze Orman.

On his CNBC TV show *"Mad Money,"* Jim Cramer will entertain you by jumping up and down and screaming like a clown as he encourages you to turn your money over to the Wall Street gangsters and banksters.

Let's start first with him, a true stock-market guru. If you were watching Cramer's *"Mad Money"* on March 3, 2008, you heard him strongly defend the financial company Bear Stearns and loudly proclaim the company was fine and you should not pull out your money.

Unfortunately, if you followed his advice, less than a week later, Bear Stearns collapsed and you lost all your money. Do you think we are being a little too harsh here? No, not really as you'll see next!!

On November 1, 2009, according to the *Wall Street Cheat Sheet,* as part of Cramer's cheerleading for Wall Street, he screamed out to his TV followers the bold recommendation to buy CIT Group. Now, you may be wondering how that worked out for his trusting audience. Well, apparently not so well, since CIT Group went belly-up, declaring bankruptcy less than 30 days later. No one knows how many of his cult followers lost virtually their entire investment listening to his brilliant advice.

Now, we don't necessarily put Dave Ramsey and Suze Orman in the same category as a Jim Cramer, as they do very good work helping people stay out of debt and manage their finances.

If you have ever actually heard Dave Ramsey or Suze Orman on radio or TV, you know they have very strong opinions regarding life insurance. They believe you should get term life insurance (renting) for a short period (10, 15, or 20 years, etc.) of time rather than getting cash value whole life insurance (buying). In a nutshell they hate cash value whole life insurance, because it can be considerably more expensive than term life insurance.

Their mantra that they love to repeat over and over again is "Buy term and invest the difference." Now, you already learned that they **borrowed** that tag line from A.L. Williams ... but, they unfortunately forgot to give him credit.

The advice and guidance from these gurus is to never buy cash value whole life insurance. They claim it is a poor savings vehicle and considerably more expensive than term insurance. Their bottom line is you simply invest the difference in the monthly premium savings in what they call quality mutual funds earning 12 percent or more on average per year. Sounds great, right?

Well, maybe not so great. Now, we are not trying to tell you that the TV and Wall Street guru's are totally wrong, just that you haven't been told the whole story. In this case the devil is in the details.

The reality is that these gurus and the so-called financial experts fail to take into account one of life's greatest realities … human nature. There was a very intriguing study done by DALBAR, **Inc.,** the nation's leading financial services market research firm.

The study was called Quantitative Analysis of Investor Behavior (QAIB). This study showed a very different picture from the one media gurus, the Wall Street hustlers, and their front men have painted for us these many years.

The study shows that over a 20-year period ending December 31, 2010, the AVERAGE equity mutual fund investor would have earned an annualized return of only 3.27 percent versus the Standard and Poor (S&P) gain of 9.27 percent. The shortfall of 5.87 percent is called the behavior gap. What this clearly demonstrates is a significant gap in performance due entirely to their own harmful behaviors. Not very impressive, was it?

In other words, as the average mutual fund investor you tend to panic when the market crashes and it could take years for you to gain back your losses … if you ever gain them back! So much for an average annual growth rates of 12 percent or more over 20 or 30 years … <u>AND THAT'S BEFORE TAXES</u>.

Let's reiterate this point as it's critical. It appears that during serious market downturns, many people tend to sell their investments in a panic. The end result according to DALBAR is it can take you years to recover your principal and your actual return on your investment is more like 3.27 percent … not the 12 percent these gurus proclaim.

Apparently when the market is doing well investor behavior is rational, however, when the stock market tanks and goes into what seems like a free fall … all bets are off.

Actually, we're not quite done yet with this subject. There is one other element of human nature especially related to their borrowed tag line of "Buy term and invest the difference." The problem is the extremely high likelihood, that you won't invest the difference. Why? Because life gets in the way! Your kids, your better half, or the fact that you will decide that money you saved is needed for something more critical.

Although those are some of the problems with their theory, there is an even bigger one. The bigger problem is term life insurance provides only a death benefit for a set term or period of time, and guess what? The vast majority of people who purchase term insurance NEVER EVER get to use it or get ANY benefit from it. The real numbers tell the tale.

Only about 2 percent of term insurance policy holders ever collect a penny from their death benefit after they paid all those premium dollars for 10, 20 or more years! Now that we got that out of the way, let's take a little closer look at these two financial gurus.

Suze Orman has estimated that her net worth is in the range of $25 million, with millions more in real estate. In between commercials for one of her big personal sponsor's TD Ameritrade, she gleefully encourages her adoring audience to invest in the stock market. What she fails to disclose is that out of her vast wealth she risks only $1 million of her own money in the Wall Street casino. Nice, right?

How about Dave Ramsey you might ask? Well, Dave has been very successful on radio and, TV and with writing books about his "Total Money Makeover" philosophy. He frequently tells his audience about his own personal bankruptcy, and because of those painful years, how he learned to live debt-free. He gives advice daily to his audience on how to achieve a debt-free life style which is certainly a wonderful goal, especially if you are stuck in credit card hell ... which is not a fun place.

As we said before, Dave and Suze believe in the "buy term and invest the difference" concept. If you listen to Dave for any length of time, you are sure to either hear a commercial for Zander Insurance or hear Dave himself recommend getting your low cost term insurance policies from Zander Insurance. We have no idea what Ramsey and Zander's relationship is, but the commissions earned by Zander insurance … must be very, very lucrative.

Dave also has a real problem with all precious metals, including gold and silver. He gets frequent calls on this subject and still bashes this as an investment in spite of the fact that gold in 2001 was about $271 per ounce and in early 2013 it was just below $1,700 per ounce. Maybe at this point it would be too embarrassing for Dave to back track from his hard line anti-precious metal stance.

Unlike Dave, many financial experts have recommended a small percentage investment in precious metals. As we discussed previously, the continuation of uncontrolled government spending will not end well, as it will cause massive inflation and dramatically decrease the value of every dollar you have. That is why a small number of gold coins or circulated silver coins could be a very prudent insurance policy for your financial safety net.

How are they right?

Suze and Dave are not totally wrong concerning the purchase of term life insurance versus permanent whole life insurance. They are correct that the monthly premium for a term life policy will be less expensive than for permanent whole life insurance.

They are also correct that many permanent whole life policies have large built-in fees, charges for insurance, and high commissions for the agents that gleefully sell you these products.

In addition, there is a problem that can potentially impact your beneficiaries if you didn't pick that great agent. The issue is that although these permanent whole life policies build up cash value, your beneficiaries will NOT receive both the cash value AND the death benefit … unless you have chosen the right agent who is both honest and knowledgeable enough to design a properly structured permanent plan.

How are they wrong?

The gurus are wrong because they made a sweeping statement incorrectly comparing term insurance with the high-cost traditional whole life policy, without properly researching the subject. They failed to explain to their adoring audiences some key facts:

The first fact is that term insurance is strictly a death benefit, while permanent whole life can be structured to have a death benefit, a cash benefit, AND living benefits you can access and utilize before you die.

The second fact is that a highly skilled and honest agent will be able to structure a unique solution for your needs using a very special type of cash value whole life insurance policy. This properly structured policy can last a lifetime while it safely grows your retirement savings.

What Dave and Suze also fail to tell you is that when you buy (rent) a term policy for a period of time such as 10, 15, 20 or 30 years, and that time is up, you have a big problem. Why? Because at the end of your term, the cost of a new term policy could be outrageously high based on your age and health condition … **assuming the insurance company would approve you for a policy … AT ANY COST!**

The most important part of what they fail to tell you is that only your highly skilled agent can find you permanent cash value whole life with a top-rated insurance company that is <u>properly structured</u> to give you the following:

- Flat premium payment throughout your life.
- Tax-free accumulation and tax free access to your money during your lifetime.
- Opportunity to achieve cash value growth, without stock market risk.
- Your principal and earned interest is never at risk.
- You can have tax free access to your death benefit to use as LIVING BENEFITS, such as:
  - In case of a terminal illness.
  - In case of a chronic illness, long term care type benefits to pay for nursing homes or home health care … in addition to your death benefit.
  - In case of critical illness, such as: heart attack, stroke, cancer, and others.

It is difficult to say why the gurus won't share this with their adoring audiences. Some have claimed it would interfere with their personal business arrangements or their lucrative side deals.

Regardless of their reasons or motivations, you will shortly learn about a unique life insurance product that can become the cornerstone of your retirement savings when structured properly and customized for you and your family.

SUMMARY

- Suze Orman and Dave Ramsey love term insurance and hate cash value whole life insurance.

- The key to success is to be your own guru by educating yourself instead of blindly following others … whose interests may be different from yours.

- With a great agent and a properly structured cash value life insurance product, you can build the cornerstone for your retirement savings plan.

CHAPTER 7: WHY ARE ANNUITIES PURCHASED?

"Tis said that persons living on annuities are longer lived than others."

— *Lord Byron (1788-1824)*

Why are people buying annuities?

According to LIMRA (an insurance industry research group), the number one reason people buy annuities is to supplement Social Security and/or pension income. It is not because the money grows tax deferred or because of product guarantees.

Many people now buy their annuities from banks, those same friendly banks who peddled CD's (certificates of depreciation) to their clients. Apparently, these banks have now miraculously changed their stance regarding the annuity and suddenly sell it as a safe vehicle to grow your money.

It is very funny that when those same banks were in competition with insurance companies, they would always emphasize that their CD's were FDIC insured. However, now that they are selling annuities, they do not seem to think this feature outweighs the fact that the average fixed indexed annuity pays 13-times more than a one-year-jumbo CD ... and almost four-times more than a five year jumbo CD!

Here is an interesting side note for you. The end result of our government's printing Monopoly money twenty-four hours a day has been to depress rates of returns on any products tied to the prime interest rates which includes CD's and fixed annuity products. Here is another interesting fact you won't be seeing in your bank's advertising.

Aside from the billions of dollars of annuities the banking industry now sells, the banks are also one of the biggest consumer's of life insurance. Many of the largest banks in the United States hold significant assets of corporate owned life insurance contracts.

It certainly seems that the life insurance and banking industries have an incestuous relationship with each other, which probably explains why the industries are allowed to coexist by the powers that be.

What is an annuity?

The simplest way to understand what an annuity is and how it works is to think about winning the lottery. If you were lucky enough to win that big prize, somewhere along the way you were asked if you wanted your millions in a lump-sum or a guaranteed payout over a 20-year period.

An annuity is a guaranteed stream of payments in return for a lump-sum investment. So in the lottery example, let's say you decide to take your millions over a 20-year payout. In essence, the lump sum grand prize deposited with the insurance company is the investment while the guaranteed payments you will receive over 20 years are called the annuity.

Annuities are an important financial tool that can be used to transfer funds out of qualified vehicles such as IRA's or 401(k)'s safely and WITHOUT taxation. They grow tax deferred; however, penalty free access is limited to 10 percent of fund value in any given year.

In most cases, withdrawals above this 10 percent threshold are subject to a surrender charge. Here is a booby trap you need to be aware of regarding annuities. The greater the return or bonus on the annuity funds deposited, the longer the surrender period ... and the surrender charges usually wipe out any bonus you receive as a result of early withdrawal.

What makes an annuity so confusing and complicated to most people are the moving parts built into the contract. There are a number of primary factors at play here that include; the way your money is credited, the time you must commit your principal, the participation rate, the penalty for early withdrawal's, etc.

As an example, in an indexed annuity, you may be credited the same percentage gain from an index (S&P, etc.) as another indexed annuity, but your *participation rate* might limit you to only 75 percent of the gain the other indexed annuity achieved.

So in that case if you were to receive an interest credit equal to $100 you would actually receive only 75 percent of that money or $75. Others may pay you a large bonus only to take it back if you do not annuitize or tell the insurance company to start paying you the principal.

The annuity market is filled with fixed and equity indexed annuities whose features and moving parts are constantly being adjusted to keep those products competitive and viable in the market place.

Moving-parts and variables include, surrender charges and bonuses, methods of interest credit, liquidity features (like early, no-penalty withdrawal of funds for LTC expenses, caps, floors, and participation rates regarding variable and indexed annuities), length of payout selected, and amount of payout selected.

Clearly, this is a complicated product that would be very challenging for you to set up yourself; it really requires the assistance of a professional insurance agent.

Many professional agents work with large brokerages that specialize in assisting agents to find suitable products and solutions for their clients. Banks work with whomever their affiliated broker provides them. Ironically, your local agent will have greater access to all types of annuity products.

So to summarize, an annuity is a popular insurance product that pays you a stream of income (taxable) and can be used as part of your retirement strategy. **So if you're looking for a guaranteed and steady stream of income or payments during your retirement, this could be a nice addition to your plan.**

Now, at this point you may be wondering what the size of your payments received from the annuity will be. Well, your payments are determined by a variety of factors, including the length of the payment period. In most annuities you decide whether you want to receive payments for the rest of your life or for a set number of years. The amount you receive will depend on the type of annuity you choose.

Although an annuity can be useful to supplement retirement, the Leeper Group prefers life insurance above annuities for a few specific reasons.

- Assets of an annuity will not pass to your heir's tax free.

- Annuity gains are subject to taxation ... unlike life insurance cash values that are available tax free.

- Annuities give you less access to your funds.

- Unlike life insurance products, annuities DO NOT have a death benefit.

What types of annuities are there?

There are two basic types of annuities: deferred and imme-diate. If you have a deferred annuity, your money is invested by the insurance company for a set period of time until you decide you want to begin taking withdrawals before or during your retirement. If you have an immediate annuity, you will begin to receive payments soon after you make your initial investment.

The immediate annuities are generally purchased as you approach your retirement age. If you have a deferred annuity, it will build up cash value from interest earned and/or a crediting strategy. When you decide to start receiving money (annuitize) from your deferred annuity, it will then be converted into an immediate annuity.

Now that you understand what deferred and immediate annuity means, there are two other terms commonly used when discussing annuities. These two terms are fixed and variable.

If an annuity is fixed, it simply means that your payout is always a fixed sum. If your annuity is variable, your payout is tied to the performance of a group of investments, the stock market, or a combination of these. So to put this in a nutshell a deferred or immediate annuity can give you either a payout that is fixed or variable … your choice.

The most popular annuity is called the Single Premium Immediate Annuity or SPIA. This is the one the lotteries use to pay a stream of payments to the winners of the big lottery prize as previously discussed. Many people use these SPIA vehicles to create a guaranteed (but income-taxed) stream of payments for a defined period of time.

There are deferred income annuities that provide you with an income stream at a later time. Variable annuities are usually related to the securities industry (Wall Street) and must be sold by licensed securities representatives, such as an Edward Jones representative.

With most securities products, your principal is at risk of loss, which is the price you will pay for a potentially higher or maximum gain. In response, some companies have provided security features, called guaranteed future account value which in turn provides a guaranteed result as specified in the contract.

Unlike the variable annuities, there are equity indexed annuities which provide the consumer insulation from stock market losses while still participating in the gains of the market with no risk to principal. These products also provide guaranteed future account values to draw from as well as a contractual guarantee that there would be no loss of principal.

The gains of many annuities are currently capped at around 2 to 3 percent. Although these gains are greater than most of the fixed return products such as CD's, they are not currently outpacing inflation. In addition, there are fixed annuities that declare a guaranteed rate of interest over a fixed period of time. There are also long term care annuities that guarantee a portion of the cash put into the annuity for costs associated with long term care type expenses.

There are several advantages to investing in annuities. All the money you invest in the annuity grows on a tax-deferred basis. The earned interest is compounded year by year on a tax-deferred basis similar to IRA's and 401(k)'s. If you have every invested dollar earning tax deferred interest, this is a big advantage over taxable investments, such as stocks and mutual funds, etc.

When you are ready to draw your cash out or **annuitize,** you have various options. You can choose to take your money as a lump- sum payment, as guaranteed payments over a set period of time, or as a guaranteed stream of income for the rest of your life. As previously stated, many retirees use an annuity in conjunction with other retirement income, such as Social Security and pension plans.

Whether your annuity is part of a qualified retirement plan such as an IRA or 401(k), or a non-qualified retirement savings plan there are certain legal benefits with your annuity. Depending on individual state laws, your annuity could potentially be protected in bankruptcy and, from creditor liens and can avoid all the red tape of probate court upon your death.

What are the disadvantages?

Although annuities sound like a perfect investment vehicle, as with your IRA and 401(k) there are some booby traps to be aware of. There are often many hidden fees and charges in the range of 1 to 3 percent a year that can eat away any of those attractive sounding profits.

In addition, your insurance agent or financial advisor can receive a hefty commission of up to 10 percent or more ... and guess who pays for that? Another booby trap related to annuities is the surrender charge. This booby trap will be especially dangerous if you pull your money out of your annuity in the first few years.

Generally, you're likely to experience surrender charges in the range of 7 to 15 percent of your account value if you leave in the first year, and the surrender charge generally declines by one percentage point each year until it goes to zero. However, be forewarned that some annuities can have even larger surrender charges as high as 20 percent in the first year ... which is another reason to use a great agent.

SUMMARY

- The annuity's primary purpose is to provide a guaranteed stream of income.

- Annuities do not require you to be in great health.

- Annuities are often used to roll over funds from a 401(k) account to avoid a taxable event.

- Some indexed annuities provide income riders that guarantee future streams of income regardless of market performance.

- The proceeds of your annuity contract could potentially be protected from attachment, garnishment, or legal process in favor of creditors in bankruptcy or legal judgment and can avoid all the red tape of probate court upon your death.

- Annuities can be used as qualified retirement vehicles.

CHAPTER 8: IUL TO THE RETIREMENT RESCUE!

"As in all successful ventures, the foundation of a good retirement is planning."

— *Earl Nightingale*

As you have already learned in this book, there are quite a few retirement investment vehicles out there that are highly recommended by the media guru's, the Wall Street elites, and many financial advisors. These include 401(k)'s, IRA's (including Roth), annuities, mutual funds, stocks, and bonds.

The indexed universal life insurance product (IUL) has become the hottest product in the history of the life insurance industry … and for good reason. It does this by addressing many of the critical issues associated with variable (securities-based products) and traditionally credited permanent life insurance policies.

The IUL was designed to protect your principal, so loss is not a problem for you, as it can be when you invest in stocks, 401(k)'s, IRA's, or a variable life insurance policy. The IUL can also offer much higher returns on your investment than traditional life insurance products. It does this by providing stock index driven returns … without you actually risking any of your money in the stock market.

This product is literally the best of both worlds, as you can achieve large gains when the stock market index goes up and protection against any loss of your principal and your gains, even when the market crashes.

All that is great, but what's even better is there are living benefits in addition to the built-in death benefit. A select number of companies offer long term care type benefits to help pay for a critical illness or the costs associated with nursing homes and home health care if you ever need this assistance.

The IUL is not a qualified plan, a Roth IRA, an annuity or even a whole life insurance plan and in our opinion, **this product enjoys more tax protections under current IRS Code than any other financial product in the market today.**

It grows money tax-deferred, allows for loan distributions tax-free and can provide a tax free death benefit. Have you heard of anything else that does all of these things?

This plan has volumes in the billions; *currently one out of five dollars saved is going into cash value life insurance plans nationwide according to LIMRA.* The reason you won't be hearing about it is that it has to be carefully structured to maximize the benefits to you and when this is done properly, the insurance agent gets a much smaller commission.

It is no wonder this very unique retirement savings vehicle is the insurance industry's No. 1 product. A properly structured indexed universal life (IUL) policy is a special type of universal life insurance that incorporates some unique features and benefits that no other plan can offer in only one product. The following are just a few of the features and benefits available to you when this product is properly structured to meet your specific needs:

- A death benefit that will pass <u>tax-free</u> to your beneficiaries.

- Your money grows <u>tax-deferred</u> AND can be accessed through <u>tax-free</u> loans.

- Keeps ahead of inflation and can be legally protected from bankruptcy or legal judgments.

- Your principal AND your gains are protected from loss.

- You can access your money at any time without penalties and it can be tax-free.

The index universal life (IUL) policy is one of the best vehicles to accumulate cash ... **and it includes a death benefit to protect those you love ... if the worst should happen.**

Although your savings and your earnings are NEVER at risk, you have an opportunity to grow your money when the stock market goes up in good times ... and in bad times when the market crashes, your savings are protected from loss!

In a correctly structured plan, you can achieve 13 percent or more with select insurance carriers when the market surges and when the market drops you have protection against the loss of your principal ... and your earnings.

In fact, with some of the top rated companies we work with, you actually receive at least 3 percent or more in interest annually even if the stock market indexes (the S&P 500, etc.) lost money for multiple years.

It is a wonderful feeling for our clients and our own families to know there is a great upside potential with these carefully structured IUL's and none of the downside potential you find with qualified plans like 401(k)'s and IRA's.

Just to make this crystal clear as to how these carefully structured IUL's operate, here is the structure. The money you put into your IUL's first pays for a death benefit. Secondly, any additional money above the death benefit payment up to a maximum amount is considered "over funding" your IUL plan ... **on a tax-deferred basis.**

The great agent, company and product will ensure that you can put in the maximum amount of overfunding allowed by the IRS without your savings vehicle becoming a "modified endowment contract" (MEC).

A MEC occurs when the cumulative premium payments exceed certain amounts specified under the Internal Revenue Code, causing your IUL to be taxed like an annuity. This is why finding a great agent is critical for your success.

If your agent does his or her job correctly and your plan is set up as a non-MEC then you will achieve the following advantages- in addition to a tax-free death benefit that goes to your beneficiaries. Your money will grow tax-deferred, and you can access your money through tax-free loans without any penalties ... even if you are less than 59 ½ years old.

Although it will seem hard to believe, these specially structured plans also include a long term care (LTC) type benefit paid out of your death benefit ... *while you are still alive!*

Associated with this LTC type benefit are two no-cost riders that allow you to receive "living" benefits. The first rider is a "chronic illness" rider that could pay for things such as a nursing home or home health care. The second rider can be used in the event of a "terminal illness" that can provide you 50 percent or more of your death benefit if you are diagnosed with a terminal illness. Some of our top-rated companies also offer a benefit In case of a critical illness, such as: heart attack, stroke, cancer and others.

Let's get down to a detailed comparison of a properly structured IUL with qualified and non-qualified plans. In figures1-3 below, you will see an apples-to-apples comparison of the IUL with the traditional retirement accounts. In figure 4, you will find a comparison of the benefits and features of an IUL with qualified and non-qualified retirement vehicles.

IUL vs. Traditional Retirement Accounts

Assumptions used in Figures #1, 2, and 3:

--30 year old male non smoker

--$500 @ month for 35 years to age 65

--8.6 percent compounded return annually for 35 years

--20-year payout at year 35 (age 65-85)

--30 percent marginal tax rate applied for all taxable funds for the 55 year duration of the illustration (age 30-85).

In order to show a clear apples-to-apples comparison these graphs illustrate the same 8.6 percent return from both IUL and the 401(k) or IRA. As you can clearly see the IUL not only performs on par with most investments, it also provides:

- Protection from market losses.
- Funds are accessible on favorable terms unlike the traditional qualified plans.
- Death benefits can now also provide for LTC expenses.
- Additionally, the funds inside IUL policies do not need to be actively monitored by you to prevent losses and ensure optimal gains, which makes these products even more attractive.
- Most importantly, indexed universal life carries a death benefit that would complete your plan (passing tax free to your heirs) should you die prematurely.

Fig. 1: Accumulated Income IUL vs. Traditional Retirement Plan:

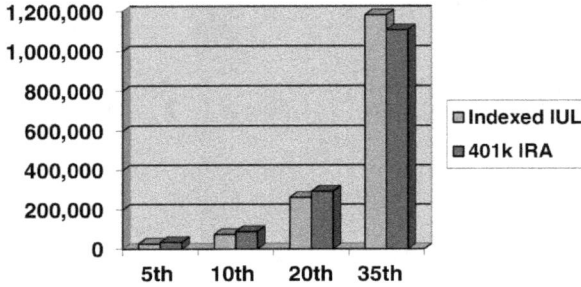

Fig. #1.

Fig. 2: Monthly Income (Age 65-85) IUL vs. Traditional Retirement Plan:

This graph illustrates you have less usable money in a traditional qualified plan because those funds will be taxed as income in the future, including the cost basis. For this illustration, we assumed a marginal 30 percent income tax rate on future distributions.

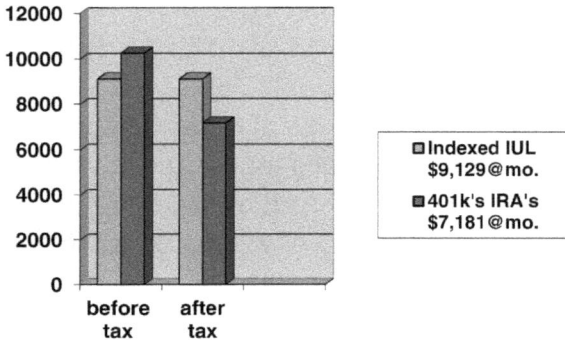

Fig. #2.

In figure #2 above, a tax of $63,000 ($1,800 a year paid from the first year through the 35ᵗʰ year, see Fig. #3) has been subtracted from the cash value of the IUL to address its taxation. This graph represents income from both vehicles over a 20-years period at 8.6 percent and at a 30 percent tax bracket.

Fig. 3: Tax Cost by Time Period-Tax Cost at Death:

Graph #3 addresses the amount of tax you would pay in both the qualified plan and IUL plan during the span of 55 years (30-85) ... **and the difference is astounding!**

The IUL assumed an additional income tax of $150 a month for the first 35 years (until age 65) while the distribution from qualified plans assumes a 30 percent tax of $2,430 paid monthly over the last 20 years for a total of $583,200.

Like the old story of the seed and the crop, consider the IUL taxation of $150 per month as taxing the seed and the $2,430 tax on the qualified plan as taxing the crop. Clearly, it is a better choice for you to have a lower tax on the seed when you are young and can afford it, versus a higher tax on the crop when you are older and can least afford it.

In the IUL there was $63,000 in taxes paid over the first 35 years (age 30-65) while you were putting in money and $583,200 paid in taxes for the qualified plan during this same period.

Therefore the tax overpayment for the qualified plan was $520,200 or 926 percent higher than the IUL. Clearly, even if you had fared better in the stock market using a qualified plan, back end taxation would wipe out your usable income.

The illustration also shows that your beneficiaries would receive $1,998,970 with the IUL as opposed to $1,275,332 for the qualified plan if you were to die at age 70. In this case, your beneficiaries would have to pay the difference of $723,638 in additional taxes with the qualified plan.

What you will find is that in most cases, when using traditional qualified plans, the government will get their taxes either while you are alive or after you die!

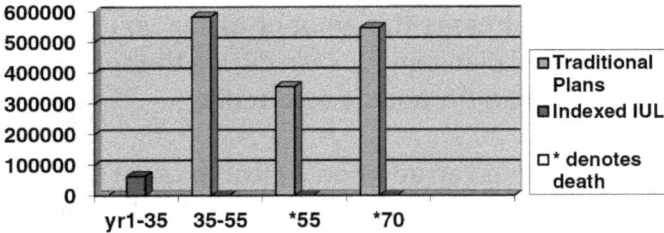

Fig. #3.

DISCLAIMER:

This is a conceptual presentation of indexed universal life performance, and no companies are represented in this illustration. The numbers and ability to participate are based on various considerations, including health, age, amounts contributed, overall stock market performance, and IUL product design. Not all carriers offer accelerated death benefits, so check with your agent for specifics regarding your policy. Life insurance should always be purchased for the death benefit as the primary consideration for having coverage.

All other ancillary benefits should be considered secondary to the death benefit. This illustration does not portray life insurance as an investment, but illustrates the generic performance of the inside build up of cash values within the indexed universal life policy vs. a traditional qualified plan using the assumptions above.

Below you will find a chart that compares the benefits and features of a "properly structured" indexed universal life plan with other retirement vehicles, such as: an indexed annuity, a 401(k), a traditional IRA, and a Roth IRA.

Our desire is to demonstrate in graphic format why we believe the IUL to be a superior product for retirement planning.

FEATURE OR BENEFIT	INDEX IUL	INDEX ANNUITY	401(K)	IRA	IRA (ROTH)
DEATH BENEFIT	YES	NO	NO	NO	NO
CONTRIBUTION LIMIT	NO	YES	YES	YES	YES
FUNDS ACCESSED TAX FREE	YES	NO	NO	NO	NO
UNLIMITED LOANS, NO REPAY REQUIRED	YES	NO	NO	NO	NO
LONG TERM CARE (CHRONIC & TERMINAL ILLNESS)	YES	NO	NO	NO	NO
RISK TO PRINCIPAL	NO	NO	YES	YES	YES

Fig. #4

At this point you may be thinking that this sounds too good to be true, and you may be wondering, why isn't everybody doing it if it's so great? Well, that's a very fair question and you deserve an answer, so here goes.

As we discussed earlier, many of the media gurus and financial planners don't get very excited over the thought of any life insurance product as a retirement vehicle. There are a few reasons for this, such as: it's just not sexy enough or they refuse to spend the necessary time to become fully educated regarding the power of this vehicle, or-in the case of financial advisors and life insurance agents, to put it bluntly ... **they don't like the smaller commissions.**

The IUL is a very flexible vehicle and can be set up with a large lump-sum payment or payments which may make this vehicle a MEC. Not to worry, in most cases you would still have a tax free death benefit for your beneficiaries and the long term care type benefits ... even if it is a MEC.

That great agent can even set up a "properly structured" IUL that is a MEC so that you can get most of the tax benefits, including tax-free loans, as long as the policy stays in force.

Clearly, the IUL is one of the best kept secrets for achieving your retirement success!

SUMMARY

- The IUL unlike your 401(k), IRA, CD or annuity has a built in death benefit that passes tax free to your beneficiary.

- A properly structured IUL can achieve a large annual cash accumulation with a cap of 13 percent or more and a 0 percent floor, meaning both your principal AND your gains are never at risk.

- Some IUL's include a living benefit such as terminal illness, critical illness and chronic illness that can provide for your long term care (LTC) type expenses ... without paying hundreds a month for a separate policy.

- A properly structured IUL can potentially be protected from attachment, garnishment, or legal process in favor of creditors in bankruptcy or legal judgment and can avoid all the red tape of probate court upon your death.

- A properly structured IUL is one of the best retirement savings vehicles for accumulating retirement cash and reducing taxes.

CHAPTER 9: HOW TO AVOID TAXES, BE YOUR OWN BANKER AND, …

"If you would know the value of money, go try to borrow some; for he that goes a-borrowing goes a-sorrowing."
— Benjamin Franklin

As you now know the deck has been stacked against you by the controllers and the elitist Wall Street gangsters and banksters. We are not talking just about restricting your pursuit of happiness by controlling what you are allowed to eat, drink, smoke, think, and say, but also what you're allowed to do with your hard-earned money.

These elites have used their bought-and-paid-for politicians and media gurus to herd you into selected investment and savings vehicles, especially the ones most profitable to them, such as the stock market, a 401(k), an IRA, a CD or a savings account.

As we demonstrated earlier in this book, there are several booby traps that can blow up your retirement and force you to outlive your money. If you do outlive your money, your choices become very slim indeed. After all your years of working and sacrificing, you now either wait in line for a government handout, beg for charity, or ask to live with your children … or, if all else fails, park your shopping cart and moth-eaten blanket next to the dumpster of a fancy restaurant.

There is an old saying that crystallizes the issue: "You can't understand the solution until you understand the problem." So just in case you forgot what those booby traps are (in addition to poor investments or insufficient retirement savings), let's review some of the biggies now:

Cost of Not Having Money

Whether you are working age or retirement age, the cost of not having money can be devastating. If you think back in your own life experiences, you'll remember that when you don't have much money, or you have bad credit or no credit at all, you become a victim and a social untouchable.

When you try to buy a house, or a car, rent an apartment, or get a credit card you will pay through the nose-with higher down payments, interest rates, deposits and/or fees. If you're lucky enough to have a bank account, your monthly fees will be higher unless you maintain a large enough balance in your account.

However, when you run out of money or you're strapped for cash, that's where the real trouble begins. Now you get ripped off with pay day loans or loans that demand your car title, and you're forced pay your bills with high-cost money orders or Western Union.

Remember, it's expensive to be poor. When you are in this situation, you pay more money for everything you need and want. Poor people always have more hassle, exhaustion and stress than those who have money. We want you to avoid this nightmare during your retirement by-making sure you never run out of money!

Banks and Banksters

Perhaps no other institution in America has the love-hate relationship with the American public that the banking industry does. Maybe you can remember how excited you were when your parents opened your first bank account with $5 so that you could learn how to save money.

Since then, many things have changed for you and for the banking industry. For one, many of the banks that were around when you were a child are no longer doing business. Hundreds of banks around the country have failed and died, as if hit by a plague.

There were a number of causes for their deaths, in addition to poor management and incompetence. These included millions or billions invested in shaky mortgage loans and their inability to confiscate your tax money through government bailouts.

These failed banks, unlike their politically connected and too- big-to-fail bankster cousins, were unable to steal your tax money so that they could repay themselves for their bad behavior, greed, and poor decisions.

The surviving banks now essentially make a living by charging you outrageous fees and nickel and diming you to death for anything they can get away with-which is quite a bit ... with government collusion!

This is evidenced by banks now making record profits based on bank, credit card and bad check fees and charges and is unlike the good old days when banks earned most of their profits from interest on your loans, their investments and loans to others using the money in your CD's and savings accounts.

This is one of the reasons so many people are replacing high-interest credit cards with debit cards and moving their business to less predatory community banks and credit unions.

The banking industry has managed almost single-handedly to alienate you and most other consumers to a point where people are now desperately trying to find new ways to meet their banking needs.

Large banks have proven over and over that they are not your friend, whether you are a struggling consumer or a small business owner. Yet millions of your fellow Americans still line up to put their money in banks that are paying them a pittance for their deposits. These same banks will gleefully charge you an arm and a leg for the use of your own funds and, as previously stated, outrageous fees for everything else.

Imagine the stress of sitting in a banker's office for a loan you desperately need. Some arrogant young punk in his three-piece suit with matching underwear pulls up your credit report and then looks down his nose at you as if you were homeless.

You probably would agree this is an unpleasant experience ... almost on the level of having a difficult root canal. So what's your alternative to the outrageous bank fees and, high-interest credit cards and bank loans, especially when your credit is not perfect? After we discuss the last booby trap, we will share that answer with you.

As we discussed earlier, you don't have to be a rocket scientist to figure out that taxes will be going up. The toxic combination of massive spending, coupled with massive debt (thanks to the inexcusable actions of corrupt politicians from both parties), can lead only to a collapse or much higher taxes.

Oh, and the worst and most devastating tax of all is a hidden tax called inflation. This tax drains the value of your money so that you will have to pay more of your dollars for everything you need or buy ... which is especially deadly during your retirement on a fixed income. Consider these several quotes that should help illustrate the problem with inflation:

> *"Inflation is when you pay fifteen dollars for a ten-dollar haircut you used to get for five dollars when you had hair."*
>
> *-Sam Ewing*

> *"Inflation is taxation without legislation."*
>
> *-Milton Friedman*

> *"Inflation comes like a thief in the night to steal your money... and your future."*
>
> *-Barry Harrin*

This hidden tax or inflation risk must be viewed over the several decades of your retirement. Historically, from 1914 until 2013, the United States inflation rate averaged 3.35 percent. In order to illustrate the danger inflation poses to your retirement, let's use a rate of 3 percent which is below the long-term average of 3.35 percent, to see what will happen to your money.

At just 3 percent inflation, your cost of living will double in 24 years. At 4 percent inflation, your living costs will double in just 18 years. Clearly this is a booby trap within another booby trap called taxes. This is a critical point, so let's make this problem crystal clear.

In this example, assume that you needed $50,000 a year to enjoy your retirement at the present time. At just a 3 percent inflation rate, in order to maintain your same life style 24 years from now, you would require $100,000 a year. However, if the government doesn't control the debt and spending and the inflation rate is actually 4 percent (or even higher), what happens to you then?

Well, remember at a 4 percent inflation rate, your living costs will reach that figure in only 18 years. So if you are 65 today, in order to maintain your same lifestyle 18 years later at age 83, you would need $100,000 a year.

To show you what a problem this is for you, here is a dramatic example. If inflation stayed at only 3 percent and you put $1,000,000 under your mattress today for the next 30 years ... your $1,000,000 would be worth only $400,000 in today's dollars.

Naturally, the higher the inflation rates the more trouble you are in. Do you think your traditional investments or your CD's and bonds will keep pace with the ravages of this hidden tax? **Not likely!**

Annual Inflation Rates Chart (2002-2012)

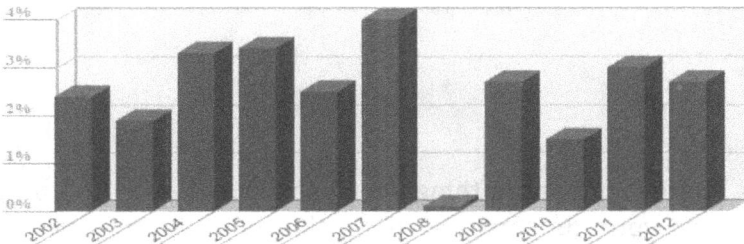

Now, before you decide to jump off the tallest building in town, there is a little good news. Since the elites and the Wall Street gangsters and banksters haven't finished plundering the American golden goose, they will be forced to keep it alive for the foreseeable future.

The bad news is that you will be helping them. How you ask? Well, you will be helping them by paying higher taxes at every conceivable level to keep their golden goose alive and laying more of those golden eggs. Nice, right!

The other bad news is that you will have a new partner in your business and your family. The ever friendly and lovable IRS and their state and local cousins will be your new business and life partners going forward ... to squeeze every penny out of you that they possibly can.

As you may have learned from the news, owing taxes or getting on the IRS's radar can make your life a living hell. Therefore, reducing your taxes has two great benefits. First, you get to keep more money in your pocket, and secondly, you reduce your exposure to the IRS ... which seems like a wonderful idea to us.

There is one more thing we want to share with you before you get your dessert and the solution to your retirement problem.

The rule of 72

If you are not familiar with or have forgotten the rule of 72, you will want to learn the power of this important rule. The rule of 72 will give you a *quick, rough estimate* of how long it takes for your savings or investment to double, based on the fixed annual interest rate you expect to receive.

To use this simple rule, just divide the interest rate you are receiving into 72. This will show you how many years it will take for your money to double. Let's look at an example together:

Using the rule of 72, how long would it take you to double your savings of $1,000 with a fixed annual interest rate of 10 percent? To get the answer, you simply divide 72 by the interest rate of 10 percent; the answer is 7.2 years.

Here is the formula: $[(72/10) = 7.2)]$. Therefore, with a 10 percent annual interest rate, our $1,000 dollar savings or investment will double to $2,000 in about 7.2 years. The chart below gives you a number of examples without having to do the math.

Fixed Annual Rate of Return	Estimated # of Years
2%	36.0
3%	24.0
5%	14.4
7%	10.3
9%	8.0
10%	7.2
15%	4.8
20%	3.6

25%	2.9
50%	1.4
72%	1.0
100%	0.7

The importance of understanding the rule of 72 cannot be overstated. It will either work for you or against you in achieving your retirement success. Let's look at some real examples to better understand this concept as you review the chart above:

- At a 7 percent interest rate, your money would double in 10.3 years.

- At a 10 percent interest rate, your money would double in 7.2 years.

In terms of real dollars, if you receive an interest rate of 7 percent with $10,000 in an account, your money would double in the 10th year and by the 20th year your account would reach $40,000. Does that make sense?

Now watch this. Let's assume your interest rate increased just 3 percent more from 7 percent up to a 10 percent interest rate. At 10 percent your $10,000 in your account would double in the seventh year to $20,000, and in that 20th year, your account would almost reach $80,000. Clearly, as demonstrated by the rule of 72, that difference of just 3 percent more interest on your retirement savings can double your money.

At this point you're probably asking how this relates to our preferred retirement savings vehicle. Well, because the cash value of our preferred savings vehicle grows tax deferred (like qualified plans) your money will actually grow much faster, because your interest is not taxed. However, as you'll see shortly our vehicle choice has many more advantages and protections than most qualified plans.

OK, now you should clearly understand the importance of a higher interest rate to double your money much more quickly. However, there is a very important related concept that very few of your fellow American's understand, and once you understand it, you can win the retirement game.

Let's say for this example you are in the 28 percent tax bracket. If you are in the 28 percent tax bracket, you get to keep only 72 cents for every dollar of income you receive. Therefore, in the previous example your annual interest rate of 10 percent is now eroded by your tax bracket of 28 percent (in this case).

Let's illustrate this point. At a 10 percent interest rate, your return after taxes on $1,000 dollars should have been $100 dollars. However, after you pay your income taxes it is now down to $72. So when you thought you were getting 10 percent interest, in reality you were getting only 7.2 percent, nearly a third less, because of taxes.

So if you get interest on non-qualified accounts such as your bank account, CD, or mutual funds, you are NOT getting the advertised interest rate, but one much lower depending on your tax rate. Clearly, this can make or break your retirement plan.

The point to take away is this: Taxes are your enemy and the enemy of your retirement. Your job is to legally get as close to a zero tax level as possible.

Still don't believe us? As in the example above, an increase of 3 percent interest (almost a third of 10 percent) doubles your money. Therefore **deferring your 28 percent tax rate (almost a third decrease) will have the same effect of doubling your money.** This is amazing stuff!

Well, you're probably ready for your dessert and want to find out how you can avoid the IRS "tax" booby trap along with the other two booby traps of "the cost of not having money" and "avoiding banks and banksters."

The answer is simple! You must take control of your destiny, lower your taxes and become your own banker, thereby making sure you never run out of money in retirement. To help you achieve this goal we needed to find you the best retirement savings vehicle available, one that offers you the most benefits and protections for the lowest cost.

Our first-place choice for this savings vehicle offers you a combination of TAX DEFERRAL, a healthy COMPOUNDED INTEREST RATE, PROTECTION OF PRINCIPAL AND GAINS and the ability for you to access your money whenever you want ... WITHOUT ANY PENALTIES OR TAXES.

Although this is a great combination, what makes it unbeatable is the addition of a DEATH BENEFIT and LIVING BENEFITS that are similar to LONG TERM CARE. As previously pointed out, in our experience, the best savings retirement vehicle to achieve all of these objectives is a "properly structured" indexed universal life insurance policy or IUL.

Although this is a great vehicle, to achieve the best results you will need to find that great agent or financial advisor. That very experienced agent or financial advisor you need should fully understand how to customize an IUL to meet your specific needs ... and should be contracted with the top IUL insurance companies that are rated A+ or higher.

If you need our assistance in setting up your own customized plan or finding a professional agent in your area, please check our contact information.

Let's be honest, many people's perception of permanent life insurance seems to be a negative one. There are a number of reasons for this perception. First, life insurance is associated with tragedy, because of its death benefit. Second, is the perceived higher cost due to excessive commissions and fees. Last is the stodgy reputation it has acquired over the past two hundred years or so.

These perceptions exist in spite of the fact that the death benefit alone has kept families out of poverty for many generations. Isn't it ironic that the thing people do not want to discuss may be the solution to their retirement concerns?

Couple this with the fact that many people do not trust the insurance companies or their agents and this has caused a real trust gap between the industry and the American consumer.

Today's permanent life insurance in the form of a "properly structured" indexed universal life insurance policy (IUL) is definitely not your father's insurance. The "properly structured" IUL is what we will be referring to from this point forward.

This IUL has a multitude of advantages, benefits and features that your father's insurance did not. It is not just a death benefit to keep your family and loved ones financially protected when you die, but also offers you outstanding tax benefits in addition to a number of "living" benefits.

In spite of the booby traps and the other curve balls life throws, the IUL can get you safely from where you are today at point A to your ultimate retirement goal at point B. An IUL savings program can be the cornerstone and heart and soul of your successful retirement strategy. This is especially true when it works in concert with your other diversified and prudent qualified and non-qualified investments.

The indexed universal life insurance policy is named for the way it credits the cash value inside your policy. Most permanent life policies have a defined way they credit the cash value of the policy. Whole life policies for example do not pay interest, but instead declare dividends that are determined by the insurance company selling the policy, based on the performance of their underlying investments.

Although universal life insurance policies pay an interest rate rather than dividends, their interest rate is also associated with the investment performance of the underlying insurance company as well.

On the other hand, the more volatile variable life insurance products are usually tied in to mutual fund or the direct performance of securities. Although the Variable life insurance products do not guarantee principal gain, they do have the potential to gain the most in a single year. However, we do not recommend this product, as this is the only life insurance product whose crediting method leaves you exposed to loss ... much like the stock market or mutual funds.

Anyone who sells you stocks, mutual funds, or variable life insurance products must have a securities license. The reason is simple. All of those products, including variable life insurance do not have a floor, and although you can make big gains there is no limit to how much of your gains AND principal you can lose.

The indexed universal life insurance policy (IUL), unlike variable life insurance, DOES NOT put your principal and gains at risk and it will allow you to receive a substantial number of benefits beyond just the death benefit.

The cash accumulation in the IUL can be very substantial as its crediting method is tied to the performance of one or more stock indexes, such as the S&P 500. However, as you will discover, your money is never invested in the stock market ... nor is it ever at risk.

Many IUL products have a built-in protection floor preventing you from ever losing either your principal or your interest gains inside your policy. Again, the interest you receive is tied to the market index of your choice with the possibility of high returns WITHOUT the possibility of loss of your principal or interest gains. This is very powerful for your retirement savings' growth and accumulation as you learned with the rule of 72.

The secret to accumulating the maximum cash and tax benefits is to get the lowest death benefit allowed by IRS regulations. A good point to remember is that life insurance is the only truly insured financial strategy.

In order to help you clearly see some of the benefits from a "properly structured" and fully funded IUL, the following are some HARD and SOFT benefits you can receive from this vehicle:

The Main Benefit:
- Death benefit tax-free
- Long term care type benefits tax-free

Intrinsic Value:
- Saving the cost of not having money
  - The "Be Your Own Banker" (BYOB) concept saves money on interest
  - Create a stream of retirement income through a TAX-FREE DISTRIBUTION
  - No bounced checks and or high-interest loans

- Zero tax strategy
  - Ability to save money on taxes as your gains grow tax-deferred
  - Zero taxes due when the death benefit is transferred to your beneficiaries

- ○ Ability to take tax and penalty-free distributions

- Accelerated death benefit
  - ○ Long term care type benefits (cash for disability, nursing homes, etc)
  - ○ Access to a portion of your death benefit if you have a terminal illness
  - ○ You have access to both your cash value and accelerated death benefits

- Legal protection from judgments related to bankruptcy or lawsuits

- Time savings
  - ○ You will save a lot of time and stress by not constantly managing a portfolio, as the IUL is a self-completing savings plan

As you can see for yourself, there are quite a few reasons to prefer the IUL over other more traditional savings or investment vehicles, whether these are IRA's, 401(k)'s, CD's, the stock market, mutual funds, or a traditional permanent (cash value) life insurance policy.

The IUL clearly gives you, the policy owner, the best of all possible worlds. This includes not just stability, growth and a death benefit, but also a multitude of living, tax and legal benefits that are unmatched by any other retirement or savings plan we have found.

We must note, however, that the IUL product will probably require future maintenance, because you, as a policyholder can make adjustments to your crediting strategy based on market conditions, the economy and your personal comfort level going forward.

As an example, if there are multiple years where the IUL is at its floor of 0 percent, perhaps it would be wise to shift some or all of the cash value into a fixed return of 4 percent until the market rebounds. Again, the assistance of a knowledgeable agent cannot be over-emphasized.

By now you should have a much better understanding of a "properly structured" IUL and how it can benefit you and your family. Now you can understand why we are so excited about this savings vehicle.

Here are a few additional retirement tips you may find both useful and interesting. An August 2012 study from the Wharton School of Business at the University of Pennsylvania found that the most critical factors to achieving retirement success are:

1. Investing early
2. Investing more
3. Retiring later

Also from that same study: "Starting to save at age 25, rather than age 45, cuts the required savings rate by about two thirds and delaying retirement from age 62 to age 70 reduces the required savings rate by two thirds. Only 7 percent of income must be saved by someone who begins saving at age 25 and retires at age 70"

It also turns out that the claimed tremendous effect of fee's, expenses and asset allocation were nothing more than urban legends in reaching retirement success. **Investing early, investing more, and retiring later will have a much more profound effect on your success than anything else!**

SUMMARY

- A "properly structured" IUL is one of the most powerful consumer tools available to you.

- An IUL will protect your principal AND your gains.

- The IUL includes both a death benefit and a number of LIVING BENEFITS, such as chronic and critical illness (heart attack, stroke, cancer, etc.), in addition to terminal illness.

- The death benefit will go to your beneficiary TAX-FREE.

- You will have access to your money with NO PENALTIES and on a TAX-FREE basis.

- A properly structured IUL can offer legal protections from attachment, garnishment, or legal process in favor of creditors in bankruptcy or legal judgment and can avoid all the red tape of probate court upon your death.

CHAPTER 10: WHAT ARE THE BEST SAVINGS STRATEGIES?

"Beware of little expenses: a small leak will sink a great ship."
— *Benjamin Franklin*

Putting It All Together

Well, now it's time to really get serious and give you information you won't find in any other retirement book. At the Leeper Group LLP we have intensely studied the retirement equation, which we view as a puzzle.

In order to make sense of this puzzle, you must learn to lower your consumer blindfold and identify the real enemies of your retirement plan. These include, the government, politicians, banksters, the media, and, of course, your high taxes and interest payments.

The pieces of the retirement puzzle are avoidable taxes and interest along with your savings and investment strategies. The variables are how much money you want for what period of time, and when this will occur.

Paying off your mortgage is not always the best move!

Traditional wisdom and the media guru's tell us we must pay off our home mortgages as soon as possible. We, however, have a different view and would like to share it with you now.

Let's all agree on a few things up front. First, home mortgage interest rates have been historically low for several years.

Secondly, it's true that by paying off your mortgage early you will significantly reduce the amount of interest you pay.

Those two facts are obvious, but what is not so obvious is what happens next. Let's say you begin paying off your mortgage early, and you have $50,000 or a $100,000 in equity in your home. This essentially means the market value of your home is $50,000 or a $100,000 higher than the mortgage payoff you owe on your home.

The problem is that this $50,000 or $100,000 equity is not accessible to you. It is what we call DEAD EQUITY, because you have no access to it unless you sell your house, pay off your first mortgage, or take out a brand-new second mortgage.

You would probably agree that most people who are happy in their homes would probably not want to sell it or take on more debt to access their equity.

Therefore, you are in a position of having no access to this DEAD EQUITY when you really need it (cost of not having money) AND that extra amount of the mortgage you are paying down is not taking advantage of the magic of compounding interest.

You already learned it is highly likely that your taxes will increase dramatically in the very near future. If you believe that this is even remotely possible, why would you want to lose your mortgage interest deduction, one of the only large deductions still available under the IRS code to reduce your taxes?

After reading this, some people may wonder if home ownership is all it is hyped up to be. They (the real estate industry) say our home equity is increasing 6 percent a year. Certainly that figure does not account for interest, income taxes paid on those monies, property taxes, insurance, inflation, maintenance, and let's not even talk about doing any home improvements.

Other than the great tax deduction, the obvious question is; how much farther ahead are you by purchasing your home? The sad truth is you would be lucky to break even.

If your house were an investment, it would probably be a poor one as your principal is tied up or unusable in DEAD EQUITY. You would also lose opportunities to make money with your money (DEAD EQUITY), and most of all, you would lose the compound effect of that money over time.

Let's be honest with each other: we all have to live somewhere. What we are paying for is the privacy and ability to call someplace our own-and you will always pay a price for that luxury. Besides, it beats living in a cave or apartment complex although those options would certainly be cheaper. As long as you don't buy into the industry hype that you are receiving anywhere near a 6 percent appreciation ... you will make the right choices!

The 6 percent the real estate industry touts sounds hauntingly familiar to the 8-12 percent that Wall Street touts. Of course these are figures these industries conjure up so they can continue to screw you!

Would you buy an expensive house if you knew up front that at best you would break even? If your answer is yes then maybe it's a good deal to have a nice place to live ... but certainly not a good deal to pay off your mortgage early as an investment strategy.

The following is a tale of two brothers that clearly illustrates the challenge and the opportunity of home ownership:

Two brothers each had purchased a $100,000 home in the same neighborhood at about the same time. They had similar incomes, credit, health profiles and a 30-year fixed interest rate of 6 percent, and they both decided they wanted to save for the future.

Andy, the older, decided he would pay his mortgage bi-weekly and put any extra money he had into paying down his home mortgage early. Best of all, his mortgage would be paid off in 24 years if he kept it up!

Paul decided to put his extra money into an IUL cash value life insurance policy instead of paying down his mortgage early. He had been very skeptical at first, but after his agent explained how his money would grow tax deferred (three times faster as seen with the rule of 72) and would also be accessible, should he happen to need it, he became much more fond of the idea.

Paul's agent showed him a comparison on paper of the difference between using his extra money to pay down his mortgage quicker versus using those same monies to buy an indexed universal life policy (IUL).

Although the comparison showed that paying his mortgage quicker would significantly reduce the amount of interest he would pay on the loan, it clearly demonstrated the overwhelming advantages of funding an IUL instead.

After reviewing the agent's illustration, Paul quickly saw how the money in the cash value life insurance would grow tax-deferred (three times faster) and at an attractive compound interest rate, and most importantly, instead of the DEAD EQUITY in his house he would have LIVE EQUITY ... to use as and when he needed it.

According to the insurance illustration, Paul would have enough saved in his cash value insurance to pay his principal off in 26 years if he wanted to do that.

Paul originally had been thinking about buying a term insurance policy for 30 years, but he realized all the extra benefits of the IUL cash value insurance made it a superior product to meet his needs.

The cash value plan not only had the same death benefit as the term policy, but it also made him his own banker with tax free access to his money. In addition, Paul would have living benefits if he ever became terminally ill, disabled, or had a chronic illness that qualified for the LTC type benefits built into his policy.

Paul asked his agent how someone would qualify for those TAX-FREE LTC type benefits built into the IUL policy. The agent explained that if it were determined that Paul was incapable of performing at least two Activities of Daily Living (ADLs) or suffered from severe cognitive impairment he would have access to the money in his death benefit.

Paul was pleasantly surprised to discover that the money in this LIVING BENEFIT would be available to pay for a nursing home, home health care, or any other expenses he had ... without the requirement that Paul sell his house and possessions to qualify for Medicaid or public assistance. Paul realized he was making a great decision by putting his extra money in the IUL versus paying off his mortgage early.

Both brothers continued about their business, and as the economy took a down-turn, both lost their jobs and were struggling to make payments on their homes in the 10th year. Unfortunately, after the older brother, Andy, fell behind a couple months on his mortgage payment, his credit score took a nose dive.

Andy didn't find this out until he went to his bank hat in hand, and filled out a credit application to secure a home equity loan. Fortunately, Andy had a lot more than the 20 percent equity required by his state to get a cash-out refinance. Unfortunately, because of his low credit score, he had to pay 8 percent to borrow his own equity.

His brother Paul on the other hand, called his agent to ask how he could obtain a policy loan on his cash value life insurance. The agent told Paul he simply needed to request from the insurance company the amount he desired as there was no credit application or approval to be sought.

Paul was happy to learn that after the fifth year he was able to take out of his insurance policy a 0 percent loan and he would still receive interest on his entire principal ... including the money he borrowed.

Although both Paul and Andy paid back their loans, Paul paid much less for his, because he did not pay 8 percent for the use of his money and also benefitted from the magic of compound interest working for him.

There was another major benefit Paul received that Andy did not. Paul was also able to take a greater mortgage interest tax deduction from his taxes than Andy over those 10 years, creating an even larger return that was also compounded in value.

As Andy now was paying back his additional loan, he no longer had the extra money to pay off his first mortgage early. He was now on track to pay his home off in 28 years rather than the 24 years he had planned on. Paul still had enough money in his cash value life insurance to pay off his house in the 26th year, but he decided to use the money for his child's college fund instead.

Both brothers died within a year of each other and still lived in the same houses when they passed. The older brother Andy had purchased a term insurance policy, but it lasted only until he was 55. Andy tried to get a new term policy, but because he had recently been diagnosed with diabetes and it ran in his family, he was no longer able to obtain coverage. He did however pay off his house and desired to give that to his child.

Paul never did pay off his house, but he still retained his mortgage interest deduction and his cash life insurance policy (and mortgage interest deduction) which had a cash value of over $200,000 as well as an additional $100,000 in death benefit.

In addition to the peace of mind of knowing he could have had his death benefit advanced for LTC, Paul was also able to travel and enjoy his retirement using a stream of tax-free income from his cash value life insurance policy. The balance of Paul's death benefit passed to his heir's tax-free, and they were able to cover their additional income taxes from the sale of his home.

College Funding and Life Insurance

Now let's look at another example with two other brothers Sam and Dean. The brothers worked at the same company making the same pay, both had children born in the same year, and both wanted to save for their kids future college costs.

Sam investigated his options and decided to put his child's college savings into a 529 college savings plan. He invested in mutual funds. He liked this option because he knew the money he set aside would grow tax deferred, as long as it was used for his child's future educational expenses.

Dean, the younger brother, also investigated his options and decided to put his money into a cash value life insurance plan (IUL) on a monthly basis. He really liked the idea that his money would grow tax deferred with the market and not be liable for taxes if he used the money for something other than educational expenses, such as a financial emergency.

Dean also knew there was no chance of losing his principal with the IUL as he had with his 401(k) by investing in stocks and mutual funds. He also liked the idea that if something should happen to him before he was able to save those funds, like a death or an LTC type event, he would still be able to fund his child's college tuition should his son choose to attend college.

As it turned out, their sons both applied to the same in-state university and also applied for tuition assistance and grants. Although both Sam and Dean made over six figures, they had their sons apply for assistance and grants because they knew people in their income bracket whose children received aid.

Unfortunately, neither boy received a scholarship; however, Dean's son qualified for tuition assistance and several grants. The reason Dean's son was the only one to receive assistance was the money he put away in the IUL could not be counted against him as an asset and therefore allowed his son to qualify for the financial aid and grants.

Unfortunately, Sam's assets within his 529 college savings plan were counted against him when his son applied. Although both brothers received tax-deferred treatment, Dean paid significantly less based on the IUL vehicle he used to accumulate his funds.

The brothers had about the same amount of money accumulated over time; however, if Dean had died prior to his son's college years, his life insurance plan would have provided for his family's needs, including his son's college. Dean's son could also have gone to an out-of-state university because he was not geographically limited by his state's 529 college savings plan.

In addition, unlike his brother's son, if Dean's son had decided not to attend college, there would not be a tremendous tax burden for Dean on the money inside his plan. Finally, should there have been a need for Dean's family to use the funds for an emergency, those funds would have been available without any penalty OR taxation which would not have been the case for Sam using his 529 college savings plan.

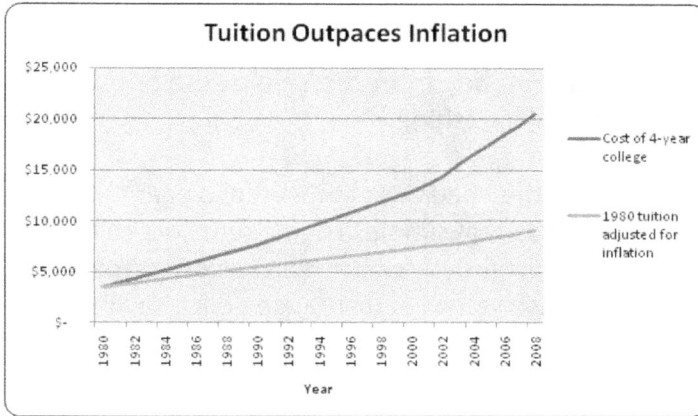

Tuition Outpaces Inflation

Mom, Dad, LTC, and Life Insurance

Mom and Dad were getting older and had just returned to their dream home from their dream cruise. All their money was tied up in their house.

The house had been appraised for over a half million dollars, and they owned it lock, stock, and barrel. Then one of the worst things that could happen did happen. Dad was diagnosed with Alzheimer's disease, and their world came crashing down.

The house they loved and looked forward to retiring in now became the main barrier keeping Dad from qualifying for Medicaid. Mom was shocked to find out that Dad's Medicare benefits would not cover nursing homes or assisted living benefits.

They were going to be forced to pay over $4,000 per month, cash, for an assisted-living facility because they owned their house and would not meet the eligibility requirements to qualify for public assistance or Medicaid.

After talking with an attorney, they even looked at getting a divorce so that they could protect the house from being sold to satisfy the Medicaid financial requirements. The other option to qualify Dad was to allow Medicaid to sell their dream home and drain all the money from the sale of the house ... **leaving Mom with virtually nothing.**

Fortunately, they had a great insurance agent. Why was he great agent? It was real simple. Their agent sold them the right policy. More importantly, it was not an accident. You see, in this situation most cash value life insurance policies will pay a death benefit only in the event of death or terminal illness

Although many life insurance policies claim they pay living benefits most pay only accelerated death benefits for the terminal illness ... but not a chronic illness or disability that would trigger an LTC type benefit. You must always check your policy very, very carefully if you don't have that great agent.

Now what makes this case really interesting is that Dad could not afford the monthly premium necessary for a cash value life insurance policy with all these powerful LTC type benefits.

Luckily Dad's very experienced agent found him a much less expensive and unique term insurance policy ... **that could be converted to any permanent plan offered by the term insurance carrier.**

His agent was very sharp and found a highly rated insurance company with a product that would fit Dad's needs. The term policy the agent found would allow a conversion to a permanent life insurance plan that included a chronic illness or LTC type rider should Dad ever need one in the future.

Once dad received his diagnosis of Alzheimer's, the agent helped Mom and Dad convert his $300,000 term life insurance plan to permanent life insurance coverage with the LTC type benefit. Unbelievably, Mom and Dad were required to make only one quarterly premium before dad was advanced $6,000 a month TAX-FREE from his $300,000 death benefit.

Best of all, because they were advancing the death benefits, future premiums on the policy were no longer due or required. The term policy they purchased had a great conversion privilege; the agent was aware of this and knew better than to sell any term product that did not. This experienced life insurance agent saved Dad and Mom from having to get a divorce or selling their dream home and forcing Mom and Dad on public assistance.

Life Insurance with Long Term Care Benefits

When Dad passed away, Mom was left with the remainder of the life insurance death benefit and a large house. They always said if anything happened to each other, the survivor would always have a free-and-clear place to live.

So, with the help of her agent, they again devised a strategy that would satisfy her future needs. Mom sold the house to her children and rented the house from them.

She used the equity in the home and part of the death benefit to purchase a paid-up (no future premiums due) cash value life insurance policy.

She did this for several good reasons: she freed up her DEAD EQUITY in the house, multiplied the value of her estate, and now had a large death benefit available to her in the event she ever needed long term care type benefits.

Mom passed away two years after Dad. If Mom had not sold the house to the kids, but had instead left it to them, the three children would have had a very unpleasant surprise.

Because the three children were, on average, in a 30 percent tax bracket, they would have received only $350,000 (minus real estate commissions, etc.) instead of $500,000 for the sale of their house. Therefore, their after-tax share would have been only $116,666 each.

After Mom sold the house to the kids, she was able to use the money she received to secure a single premium life insurance death benefit of over $1 million, which she passed to her three children income-tax free. Each of the three kids received $333,000 tax free as opposed to $116,666 after paying taxes on the sale of Mom's house.

If Mom and Dad had not purchased that term policy, the three kids would be splitting up their debt from long term care expenses as opposed to their assets. Thank goodness for the agent who sold the right product! There is no way to measure the value of a knowledgeable agent and how he or she can be of service to you.

Just a Side Note on LTC:

Many consumers are simply not aware of this potentially devastating issue. This is evidenced by the fact, that roughly 23 percent of those recently surveyed said they have no plans to address LTC for themselves, according to a Nationwide Financial Survey recently conducted with consumers ages 50 and above.

The survey also indicated that 22 percent think they will fund future LTC expenses with their 401(k) and 21 percent would fund it from their personal savings.

In addition, 64 percent of those surveyed did not believe states could force children to pay for their parents medical bills. According to the following article, this is a growing trend that could be adopted by many more states in the future. Although an unpopular topic of discussion, it is a subject that deserves your full attention while you have the facilities to address it.

This subject was covered in a June 22, 2012 Wall Street Journal article by Kelly Green. The article pointed out that 29 states have "Filial Support" laws that could be used to go after adult children's wallets to pay for their parents' unpaid LTC bills.

Those states are: Alaska, Arkansas, California, Connecticut, Delaware, Georgia, Indiana, Iowa, Kentucky, Louisiana, Maryland, Massachusetts, Mississippi, Montana, Nevada, New Hampshire, New Jersey, North Carolina, North Dakota, Ohio, Oregon, Pennsylvania, Rhode Island, South Dakota, Tennessee, Utah, Vermont, Virginia and West Virginia.

Don't get too happy if your state is not on the list, as Medicaid is one of the fastest-growing and out of control expenditures for the states ... **and they will probably ask for your help to fund it soon!**

Hedge Fund Strategy

Although this is a very exotic and complicated-sounding term, it is really necessary for you to be aware of this concept. First, what is a hedge fund? Most hedge fund investment strategies aim to achieve a positive return on investment regardless of whether markets are rising or falling. These are closed funds that are not available to the retail public.

A few years ago Paul Leeper showed his sons the power of this concept. He had two dimes in his hand. He proceeded to tell the boys that in 1964, before they were born, these two same dimes would pay for a gallon of gas.

As the boys took a closer look at the dimes, they noticed that both dimes were pre-1964; they knew they were worth a lot more than the face value, as the coins had 90 percent silver content. He then explained that these two dimes today if sold for the silver, could buy that same gallon of gas as was the case 49 years ago.

Even though, "hedge funds" are not available to regular people, the underlying concepts and objectives of the product are. The concept behind this sophisticated financial product teaches us some important things we can do ourselves to offset things we have no control, over, such as inflation.

Will the dollar continue its downward spiral as a result of the U.S. government's money-printing policies? How much return on the dollar can you count on receiving when the underlying currency is dropping in value?

One of the greatest features of a properly structured life insurance policy is the ability to use the money inside the contract for whatever purpose you desire. What better use could there be for your money than to protect it against the devaluation of the dollar or inflation?

Here is a technique some people have used to accomplish that: They took out a policy loan and bought physical precious metals with the funds. Normally, when the dollar goes down in value, the value of the metals goes up. So if they had $10,000 in gold and the dollar dropped in value, the gold would appreciate and provide a greater number of dollars. In the meantime, they will make up the difference while everyone else's account is depreciating from a weak dollar.

Sometimes you hear about people investing in gold through the stock market, by buying paper shares that are backed by precious metals. Often times these products are packaged in what is termed "exchange traded funds." Although there are profits to be made when the value of these shares goes up, these products do not have the same intrinsic value as owning a liquid commodity like gold or silver.

If you were to buy a physical commodity like 100 ounces of silver worth $3,000 and the price went down from $30 to $25 an ounce, you would still have 100 ounces of physical silver and would not have lost an ounce even though the dollar value is at $2,500.

On the other hand, if you bought some exchange traded funds and lost this value, you would have only your funds in your account full of inflationary dollars and would not have anything physical in your hand to back up the value of your dying currency!

The following is a chart showing what happened to both the dollar and gold between 2001 and 2010.

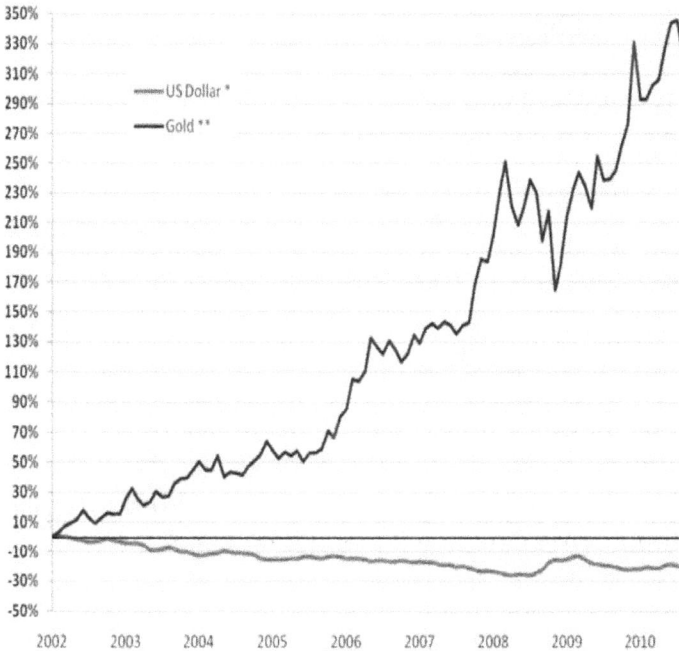

Strategies for Funding Yourself and Your Grand Children #1

Dan and Ann are 65 years old and know about inflation. Although their kids are doing well, they are worried that the cost of higher education for their grandchildren could be beyond their children's reach. Dan and Ann have five grandchildren, and they would like to leave a small legacy for their grandchildren's college funds.

The couple has assets, but worry they could possibly need the funds themselves for their own long term care costs. Their financial planner recommended a generation-skipping IRA but, it provided no access for LTC expenses without substantial tax consequences. After reviewing all their options and because their health was good, they decide to purchase a life insurance policy to meet their objectives.

After meeting with their highly recommended agent, they purchased policies that included a LTC type rider for both of them in addition to a death benefit for their grandchildren. The money they used to pay for the insurance came from their retirement savings of approximately $150,000. They purchased the policies over a ten-year period for a premium of $14,000 for both policies annually.

As a result, Dan and Ann both had an approximate $338,000 fund to draw from, $153,000 for him and $185,000 for her. The death benefit on both policies had a provision to accelerate the death benefit to pay the costs of LTC.

Their heirs (the grandchildren) would receive a total of $338,000 tax-free as opposed to leaving them $150,000 savings for which the grandchildren would be fully taxed when Dan and Ann died.

So if Dan and Ann did not need LTC, the grandchildren would be able to divide their $150,000 savings five ways upon their death, which is $30,000 each. That $30,000 would be taxed based on the grandchildren's respective tax brackets. If the heirs or grandchildren were in a marginal tax bracket of 25 percent they would receive $23,500 as an inheritance, whereas with properly structured life insurance policies, their grandchildren would each receives $67,000 a piece … **without ANY income taxes due.** Therefore the gift amount was increased a whopping 285 percent after tax considerations.

Some might say at this point that they spent $140,000 over a ten- year period, which would wipe out their $150,000 savings account. Keep in mind that some of the monies have been going into cash value inside the policies, so after 19 years, the couple would still have $134,000 in cash value after paying the total life insurance premiums of $140,000. So how much did they really spend to put this concept in place in the past ten years? The answer is $6,000 over a ten-year period for both. In the 20th year, the policies would have over $172,000 in cash values built up even though Dan and Ann stopped making the premium payments at age 75.

At this point the insurance would have a net gain of $32,000 and still have a secured death benefit of $338,000 for both Dan and Ann. On the other hand, should one or both need long term care at a current cost of $4,000 a month, their savings would have lasted 18 months for one person's care and nine months for the care of both.

Should this event occur, the grandchildren would receive nothing and depending on the state in which they reside, Dan and Ann's kids could be held responsible for any of their healthcare costs that exceeded their assets. Life insurance would increase the usable assets for possible long term care expenses.

Strategies for Funding Yourself and Your Grand Children #2

Betty is a 67 year old grandmother who, unlike Dan and Ann lives on a fixed income and has a very modest amount of savings. She had two grandchildren whom she adored. One day, after learning about the idea from one of her friends, she decided she would look into life insurance as a way to give a small gift to them upon her passing.

Betty's friend recommended a great insurance agent she had worked with for a number of years. Betty met with the agent who completed a fact finder on Betty. The fact finder took into account her financial situation, her costly Medicare health plan and her desire to do something for the grandchildren. They scheduled two separate appointments, one for her Medicare supplemental insurance and the other to find a life insurance plan that met both her needs and budget.

In their first meeting the agent found Betty a similar type Medicare supplement to the one she had, but at a savings of about $100 a month. Needless to say, Betty was pleased. However, she was even more pleased at the second meeting when her agent showed her a cash value life insurance plan that provided a death benefit of $25,000 for only $57 a month based on her age and health status.

The life insurance plan allowed Betty to achieve her objective of giving her grandchildren a small gift upon her death, and as a bonus, an extra $43 a month in her bank account.

A great question at this point is, what if, due to Betty's health, she couldn't qualify for a life insurance policy, what would happen then? This is a very important question for both grandparents and parents that might not be able to qualify for a life insurance policy due to their health conditions. Here is an interesting strategy.

Policies purchased on the lives of the grandchildren are referred to as juvenile policies. Some grandparents who are uninsurable will buy a small cash value policy for their grandchild that accumulates cash value inside the policy tax deferred and compounded.

In this situation, the life insurance benefits in these policies' would be received through the cash value of the policy, not the death benefit of the insured. In this case, the grandparents are the owner's and payers of the policy, and the grandchildren are the insured on the policy.

The life insurance policy can be owned by the grandparents, parents, children or another related party. The amount of money you can deposit into these policies is related to the death benefit. The death benefit for juvenile policies is limited, so the ability to give larger gifts or fund college is more challenging using these juvenile policies. So here is another possibility if you are seeking those larger gifts or funding.

Grandparents can purchase a life insurance policy on the lives of their children as opposed to the grandchildren whose funding is limited due to the low death benefit. Naturally, if allowable, a larger death benefit would provide a greater amount of cash available for funding, if that is your objective.

Small Business Retirement Planning and Life Insurance

Dr. Rodriquez's practice was thriving and because of that she was now in a position to design her retirement plan at age 50. An analysis showed the doctor that by contributing $5,000 a month for only 10 years (a total contribution of $600,000) she would have a $1.2 million death benefit. Now, if you think this can't possibly apply to you, simply remove a zero and you can see how it may work for you and your situation.

By the 20th year, she is conservatively projected to receive $130,000 a year for the next 20 years. So if you were to remove a zero, you would receive $13,000 a year for 20 years and would have contributed only $60,000 over ten years. Now, this is, of course, based on her health class and age and gender, all of which play into the ultimate numbers.

A properly structured IUL allows Dr. Rodriguez the tax-free use of her funds and is the primary way she can avoid the cost of not having money as discussed in previous chapters.

So at age 70, she will reach the coveted 0 percent tax bracket. This will be very important for her, because much of what she makes over a lifetime will go towards taxes if she does not have a plan to avoid them.

Let's assume Dr. Rodriguez's current tax rate on her income is 39 percent. Dr. Rodriguez would need $211,900 a year on a pretax basis to match the after-tax amount of $130,000 a year retirement benefit from her IUL. In order to determine the pretax amount required to fund the after-tax amount of $130,000 (or any amount) use this formula:

Tax rate = 39 percent

100% - 39% = 61%

61% / 100% = 1.63%

1.63% x $130,000 = $211,900

This means if Dr. Rodriguez didn't have her IUL, she would either have to contribute significantly more for the same amount annually or take significantly less out for the same amount put in.

The savings generated in the IUL by having use of those funds, the interest saved as those funds grow, and the compounded effect of the saved interest and taxes all work together on the cash value side of the policy. **The icing on the cake is for Dr. Rodriguez to be able to take her distributions tax free.**

On the other hand, if she went to see her broker and invested $5,000 a month in the stock market and did not die or need LTC, she would have a pretty tidy sum, right? It might seem that way because she would have more money if there were no life insurance expenses involved right? Wrong! If she had 40 percent more, she would have to pay taxes on that additional amount, which would actually make her higher account value worth less in terms of usable dollars as she would have to pay taxes on that money.

In addition, Dr. Rodriguez will also receive a smaller amount from her 401(k) and Roth IRA that is under the threshold of taxation, because the amount projected is lower than her standard deduction and personal exemption at retirement.

So in essence, Dr. Rodriquez will qualify to be in the coveted 0 percent tax bracket. She will receive her entire retirement income tax free! The qualification to be in this 0 percent tax bracket does not require money; it requires planning and knowledge and most of all ... the right agent!

Throughout this book, cash value life insurance is referred to as a "tax-free" financial vehicle based on the following tax attributes: income-tax-free death benefit, tax-deferred accumulation of policy values, and tax-free access to basis.

Policy loans in excess of basis are income tax-free so long as the policy remains in force. This assumes the policy is not a modified endowment contract (MEC). Loans taken directly from the policy will reduce the death benefit.

To appreciate the benefits of the 0 percent tax bracket, we begin by defining the three basic types of investment buckets: taxable, tax-deferred, and tax-free.

The Taxable Bucket:

This consists of investments such as money markets, CDs, stocks, bonds, and mutual funds. Generally speaking, investors pay taxes on these investments every year as the investment grows. From a tax-efficiency perspective, therefore, balances in this bucket should be just the right amount. Any surplus accumulation should be systematically shifted into the tax-free bucket.

The Tax-Deferred Bucket:

Because the tax-deferred bucket is taxed at ordinary income rates upon distribution, it is the bucket most impacted by the rise of tax rates over time.

The Tax-Free Bucket:

To understand the virtues of the tax-free bucket, we must begin by defining what constitutes a tax-free investment. To be truly tax-free, there are two qualifications: First, it must actually be tax-free. That means free from federal, state and capital gains taxes. Second, distributions from this bucket should not count against the Social Security tax threshold of which we previously spoke. As a caveat, municipal bonds, widely renowned as tax-free investments, fail on both counts. What does that leave?

Bucket #1 - Roth IRA

- Contributions up to basis (Cost basis means the principal or investment before any returns) can be withdrawn before the age of 59 ½ tax-free with no penalty after five years.

- Growth on contributions can be withdrawn tax-free after reaching the age of 59 ½.

- Distributions do not cause social security to be taxed.

- There are no required minimum distributions (RMD) at age 70 ½.

- Clients can contribute $5,000 per year, or $6,000 per year beyond age 50.

Bucket #1 (a) - Traditional IRA

- (Up to the standard deduction and personal exemptions), and Social Security.

Bucket #2 - Cash Value Life Insurance:

- Tax-Free (withdrawals up to basis and 0 percent loans thereafter).

Bucket #3 - Social Security:

- Tax-free (Distributions from the Roth IRA), cash value life insurance, and the traditional IRA [at the above-mentioned levels] do not affect the income threshold where Social Security becomes taxable.)

By taking distributions from these three pools of money, you can attain the coveted 0 percent tax bracket.

Retirement Buckets

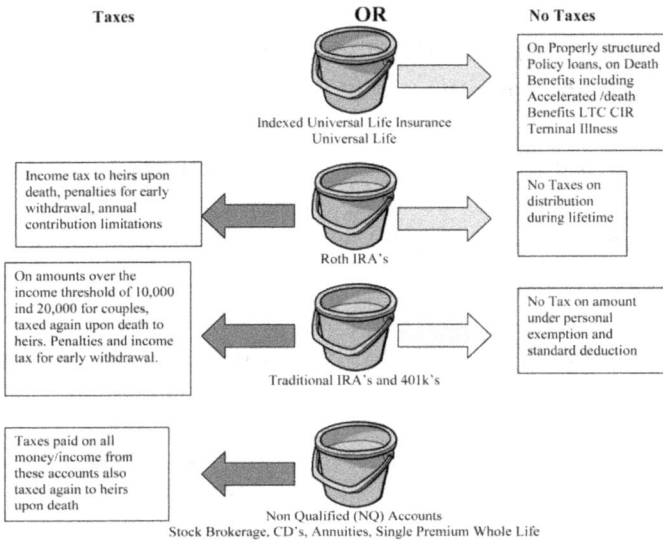

| Taxes | OR | No Taxes |

Indexed Universal Life Insurance
Universal Life

On Properly structured
Policy loans, on Death
Benefits including
Accelerated /death
Benefits LTC CIR
Terminal Illness

Income tax to heirs upon
death, penalties for early
withdrawal, annual
contribution limitations

Roth IRA's

No Taxes on
distribution
during lifetime

On amounts over the
income threshold of 10,000
ind 20,000 for couples,
taxed again upon death to
heirs. Penalties and income
tax for early withdrawal.

Traditional IRA's and 401k's

No Tax on amount
under personal
exemption and
standard deduction

Taxes paid on all
money/income from
these accounts also
taxed again to heirs
upon death

Non Qualified (NQ) Accounts
Stock Brokerage, CD's, Annuities, Single Premium Whole Life

Bonus Section:

How Network Marketing (MLM) Can Work for You:

From the time they were kids, Ray and Dale Leeper remember their dad Paul Leeper constantly joining various network marketing ventures or multi-level marketing companies (MLM's).

In the beginning, the boys (like all boys) just did what their dad did, not truly understanding all of his reasoning. Over the years, Paul traveled frequently, making it a point to combine tax deductible events with his recreational pursuits.

The boys remembered clearly when their dad bought an RV, deducted it from his income tax, and traveled across the United States. He put a business sign on his RV and took his network marketing venture on the road with him. All the way down the road he paid less because it was discounted by his tax bracket percentage. He joined international network marketing companies when traveling abroad, as he understood the tax system.

Ray, the older of Paul's two sons, was curious after he heard his mom and dad talking about both network marketing and a trip they had just taken to Japan. Ray was puzzled and couldn't understand how his parent's' skin care network marketing business could be related to that trip.

Paul explained to his curious son that his network marketing organization was an international company needing business partners around the world, including Japan. When Paul and his wife (official interpreter) went to Japan and approached her relatives to recruit them for the MLM company in Japan, the trip became tax deductible ... even though the relatives declined to join.

Paul's exact reply was a classic: "We flew there; your mother (official interpreter) asked them (Japanese relatives) if they would like to join, they said no thanks and we wrote off the trip." The following quote illustrates how our system really works.

> *"There are two systems of taxation in our country, one for the informed and one for the uninformed."*
> — **Honorable Learned Hand,**
> **Federal Judge U.S. Court of Appeals**

Before you dismiss network marketing as not for you, look seriously at some of the tax benefits this type of business could provide you and your family!

The two systems of taxation really refer to those with business tax deductions and those without business tax deductions. Network marketing provides a proven, low-cost way of establishing legitimate tax deductions. Besides that, who knows? You may strike it rich in that business in addition to the obvious tax advantages.

One must think outside the box to prepare for retirement, and this strategy is certainly one you will not be reading about in any other financial or retirement book.

How would a network marketing (MLM) business fare against a part time job?

Depending on your job, there would be expenses like clothing, dry cleaning, lunch, gas, and other related transportation expenses, all of which are not tax-deductible from an individual standpoint. Any income you receive as an employee of a company would be received after tax.

The MLM opportunity allows for the tax deduction of part of your home and utilities for business expenses related to your home-based business. It allows you to pay your kids to perform business-related tasks on a tax-deductible basis and an extra tax deductible allowance for your kids.

The MLM also allows for tax deductions related to the use of your vehicle for business purposes as well. Remember, you are now ahead of the game and you still have not made a penny in your business. Because of the inherent tax benefits you receive by having your own business, you are virtually guaranteed to succeed, from a tax stand point. Naturally, you should always seek the appropriate legal, tax, and professional advice before taking advantage of any business opportunity.

Some may consider the suggestion of joining an MLM opportunity distasteful advice; however, it is certainly not as distasteful as dealing with pay day lenders, pawn shops or title lenders and other predatory businesses'. It is simply another tool available to you for reducing your tax burden and potentially building a home-based business.

SUMMARY

- **Paying off your mortgage is not always the best move!**

- **Cash value life insurance may be your best bet for college funding.**

- **An IUL offers the advantages of having LTC type benefits and avoiding public assistance through your cash value life insurance.**

- **Hedge fund strategies can help your retirement.**

- **How starting a part time business can help get you to that elusive 0 percent tax bracket.**

CHAPTER 11: BUT I DON'T HAVE ANY MONEY!

"Ever wonder about those people who spend $2 apiece on those little bottles of Evian water? Try spelling Evian backward."

— *George Carlin*

You might be thinking at this point, "I really want to do the things you suggest, but I don't have any extra money to get an IUL or an annuity."

This has been a common theme we have heard from many of our readers and clients. The reality is that our devastating economy has caused too many people, to pull back on their retirement plans. Many of these people after reading our book tell us they desperately want to get started right now, but they can't because they are living paycheck-to-paycheck.

The truth of the matter is this: More than 75 percent of Americans are now living paycheck-to-paycheck, according to a survey released in June of 2013 by Bankrate.com. Unbelievably, that means that three out of every four American's could be only one or two paychecks from a financial disaster.

Sounds pretty depressing, right? Well, before you reach for that bottle of tranquilizers, give up on your retirement plans, and search for a four-star homeless shelter, give us a few more minutes to set things straight.

You already learned why the country is in such terrible financial shape, but what about the three of every four American's living paycheck-to-paycheck?

You may be wondering why you should even care about this. Well, the reason you should care is you will need to partner with that experienced agent or financial planner to reach your financial and retirement goals.

The average, run-of-the-mill insurance agent or financial planner will not be any help to you because they are looking for clients with big bucks ... because big bucks mean big commissions or big fees for them.

So again, you must be prudent in choosing that insurance agent or financial advisor. At our agency we prefer working with and spending our time helping middle-class individuals and small- business people. Yes, the commissions are a lot smaller, but our personal satisfaction is greater ... and so are the referrals we receive to their friends and family.

If you fall into this middle-class group, the first thing we do to help you is simply work to understand your current financial and personal situation and what you would like to do after you retire. We start the process by helping you do some individual and family soul-searching.

This individual and family soul-searching is accomplished by using our Fact-Finder Process. This question-and-answer process will help you discover what has been happening to you in the past and the present and can project your future financial condition. It is an amazing process, and the results can be astounding.

Here are some of the revelations that have come out of many of our fact-finding sessions with clients who were having trouble saving money for the future or even building an emergency fund.

The common theme we discovered in our fact finders, believe it or not, is that <u>many people have come to believe that luxuries are essential expenses!</u>

Let's look at some specifics. If you think back to the not so distant past, buying a new house and a new car was a true luxury. Now, people are in a bind because they bought that beautiful new house they couldn't afford.

The same goes with new cars they couldn't afford: the always friendly salesman convinced them they could handle the payments ... if they just stretched it out over seven years.

Unfortunately, that same friendly salesman forgot to tell them that the moment they drove off the car lot, their shiny new car would lose 30-40 percent of its value, and their auto insurance bill would go through the roof.

If you think back a bit, you may recall that cable TV with every channel known to man was considered a luxury, as were the Internet, the latest iPad and smart phone. Now, even people on government assistance believe it their right to have these things ... along with a 50 inch flat screen and a DVR. Is it any wonder so many of us live paycheck-to-paycheck?

Then, of course, we have a number of luxuries we just have to have to keep up with the Jones's. These can be everything from over-the-top weddings, vacation homes, time-shares, boats, jet skis, exotic vacations, and cruises.

Unlike our parents and grandparents, how many of us now go out to eat two or more times each week? The cost of feeding a family of four at a restaurant such as Olive Garden can easily approach $100 with a tip included.

Then we have the overspending on groceries, new clothes, sports equipment, and must-have electronic toys and games. Clearly, buying store-brand groceries and all the rest at discount stores, Amazon.com or eBay will save you big bucks.

After discovering all of this lost money during the client fact-finder process, our group decided to try an experiment. We each used the Fact-Finder Process on each other. The results were very interesting.

In spite of our experience in this area, we discovered that those of us with two or more children were overspending by anywhere from $500 to $700 per month ... wasting money that could be better used for college, emergency and retirement savings. This amount did not include any monies received from federal tax refunds. How much extra cash do you think you could find in your own family?

Clearly, this $500-$700 that we were misspending or wasting each month does not include all the money that could be saved on income taxes and interest on loans. Remember, when you become your own banker, you get to slash your taxes and the interest on your loans.

Also, don't forget the "DEAD EQUITY" in your house that can be accessed by not rushing to pay off your mortgage early and instead using that money and all the other savings to fund an easily assessable IUL.

Until we do a fact finder, most people have no idea how much money will slip through their fingers and be lost forever ... when they really need it most.

Most of us also don't realize how much money we really make and how little we really end up with. If you're still skeptical let's look at an example.

Take a typical couple in their early forties with two children and an annual household income of $80,000. Assuming they work another 25 years, some simple math shows us that this couple will earn about $2 million.

That sounds like a lot of money to most everyone who reads this; however, during those 25 years, that typical American couple will spend almost all of their $2 million in earnings.

How, you ask? By paying their monthly bills, giving hundreds of thousands to the IRS in income taxes, interest on loans, prepaying their mortgage, and untold thousands wasted *on all the luxuries they considered essential.*

The bottom line here is, we don't want you to make the same mistake as the typical American family living paycheck-to-paycheck and retiring with only Social Security ... **that is, if Social Security still exists in the future.**

SUMMARY

- **Luxuries are NOT essentials!**

- **Paying off your mortgage is not always the best move!**

- **An IUL may be your best bet for an emergency fund, college funding, and LTC type benefits.**

- **You do have the money to fund your own retirement … you just need to find it!**

CHAPTER 12: A SENSE OF URGENCY!

"Be willing to make decisions. That's the most important quality in a good leader. Don't fall victim to what I call the Ready-Aim-Aim-Aim Syndrome. You must be willing to fire."
— *Russell H. Ewing*

Paul Leeper retired from the Air Force at an early age (38) and took with him the discipline and life lessons he learned from the military. In order to teach an important life lesson to his sons, Paul told them a story he picked up in the military.

The story was about a general Paul had worked closely with: The general had told Paul behind closed doors about his frustrations regarding the way things were currently being done in the Air Force.

The general asked "Do you know what we're missing here Sergeant Leeper?" To which Paul courteously replied "No Sir!" The general said "What we are missing here is a SENSE OF URGENCY!" *The general knew that urgency translated to action and those actions created results!*

This is the reason Paul told anyone he met to buy as much life insurance as they could, when they could, because their health would one day prevent them from doing so.

He warned his agents that an overreaching and encroaching government could take away the great tax advantages that cash value life insurance currently provides to its owners.

Paul drilled into his professional agents that approximately 95 million adult Americans are without life insurance and those families could be financially destroyed if a bread winner were to die without sufficient life insurance coverage.

He told them they had a responsibility and should have a sense of urgency to help as many people possible to take advantage of the great benefits of a properly structured cash value life insurance plan ... **while those benefits still exist.**

AIM HIGH

During Paul's tenure in the Air Force, he worked in the Directorate of Advertising and was part of a team that created the AIM HIGH advertising campaign for the Air Force.

His sons had asked him what they meant by AIM HIGH. He explained a term called "Kentucky Windage" to them to define the real meaning of AIM HIGH.

"Kentucky Windage is when you make an adjustment in your aim for the wind affecting your target." The term "Aim High" had a similar meaning because if you "Aim High" you will often compensate for other factors that may affect your shot, such as sights or wind. So by setting your goals high, even if you were to miss your mark, you will have still exceeded your lower expectation.

We have provided you with the information, strategies and concepts, but you are solely responsible for your own high expectations. We close by asking you to Aim High with your goals so that even if you fall short, you will still be ahead of the retirement game!

ONE LAST POINT:

As you may have heard many times in the past, you need to have a legal will. Even if you have a will now, if your will is from a previous marriage or more than several years old, you should have it updated. You might be thinking at this point, "Why do I need a will?"

Getting a legal will is one of the most important things you can do for those you love. Having this document will ensure your property, personal belongings, and other assets will go to whomever you wish. It is an absolute necessity to have a will if you have minor children, as this is the place where you can name a guardian for them ... rather than letting your state make that decision for you.

If you die without a will, the intestacy laws of your state could very well dictate how your estate is divided and who will receive shares. Even if you have a small estate, this process can be long and very costly to those you love. Having a legal will can prevent these problems for your family and friends and keep them from fighting it out in probate court over who gets what from your estate ... even if it's a small one.

We hope you have received many new concepts and ideas in our book that you will find beneficial to you and your family in these times of financial uncertainty. The only thing left for you to do now is to aim high and have a sense of urgency in taking action to protect yourself and your family.

If you enjoyed our book and would like our assistance in setting up your own customized retirement solution, or you would like to find a qualified professional in your area, please feel free to use the contact information below.

AUTHORS	EMAIL
Barry Harrin	comanchepress@gmail.com
Raymond Leeper	raymond@leeper.com

AUTHORS	WEB SITE
Barry Harrin	www.harringroup.com
Raymond Leeper	www.leeperllp.com

SUMMARY

- **Have a sense of urgency!**

- **Aim high to ensure you hit your retirement target.**

- **Make sure you have an updated will.**

- **Take action today to protect yourself and your family from financial crisis and the unexpected … <u>BEFORE IT HAPPENS!</u>**

RECOMMENDED READING

- *Richest Man in Babylon*, by George Samuel Clason

- *Think and Grow Rich*, by Napoleon Hill

- *Fund Your Future,* by Ed Slott

- *Brain Droppings*, by George Carlin

GLOSSARY OF TERMS AND ACRONYMS

401(k): A tax-deferred savings and investment plan in which employees may choose to contribute up to a set amount each year. Employers often match a percentage of an employee's contributions. Employees control how the assets are allocated among different types of investments. All taxes plus a 10 percent penalty are usually imposed on withdrawals made before age 59 ½.

403(b): Similar to the 401(k) plan, but generally offered by nonprofit organizations instead of for-profit businesses. It allows contributions from employees to grow on a tax-deferred basis until they are withdrawn. At withdrawal, the funds are subject to tax like ordinary income.

457 Plan: Named in reference to the portion of the Internal Revenue Code that defines its basic rules, the 457 is a tax-exempt deferred compensation program provided to employees in state and federal governments and agencies. While similar to the 401(k) plan, the 457 plan never receives matching contributions from the employer, nor does the IRS consider it to be a qualified retirement plan.

Accidental Death Benefit: In a life insurance policy, benefit in addition to the death benefit paid to the beneficiary, should death occur due to an accident. There can be certain exclusions as well as time and age limits.

Activities of Daily Living (ADL's): is a term used in healthcare to refer to daily self-care activities within an individual's place of residence, in outdoor environments, or both. These include: Bathing, preparing and eating meals, moving from room to room, getting into and out of beds or chairs, dressing, using a toilet.

Actuary: The individual who uses statistical mathematics to calculate the premiums, dividends, reserves, and pension, insurance and annuity rates for an insurance company or other institution involved with fiscal risk.

Adjusted Gross Income (AGI): The amount of income obtained after subtracting allowable adjustments from the total income received. These adjustments include contributions to an IRA, paid alimony, moving expenses, and contributions to Keogh accounts.

Annuitant: The individual who receives payments from an annuity plan under the terms of that plan.

Annuity: - A contract that guarantees fixed or variable payments over time. Some investors buy annuities to provide them with a stream of income in the future.

Annuitization: The process of converting an annuity contract's value into an income stream represented by periodic payments made over a specified period of time.

Accelerated Death Benefits: Allows for the policyholder to receive their benefits before death, usually in cases of terminal illness or need for long-term care.

Arbitrage: The act of buying and selling commodities in two markets at the same time to benefit from price differences between the markets. This can also be an investment or trading strategy often associated with hedge funds.

Beneficiary: The individual or legal entity receiving a life insurance or annuity death benefit when the insured designated in the contract dies. Typically this is a child or spouse. The beneficiary cannot manage the annuity — a right reserved solely for the contract owner.

Bond: A form of debt created by an institution that wants to borrow money. Buyers of bonds receive periodic payments of interest, with the principal amount of the bond typically repaid as a lump sum by a specified date.

Buy-Sell Arrangement: An arrangement designed to dispose of an interest in a business when the business's owner retires, becomes disabled, or dies.

Be Your Own Banker (BYOB): The ability to *bypass* banks, finance and credit card companies and become your *own* source of financing.

Cash Value (Also Surrender Value): The amount available in cash for loans and/or withdrawals. Accessing Cash Value may reduce the death benefit and may increase the risk of lapse.

Cafeteria Plan: An employee benefit plan that provides flexible dollars to be used by employees to pay for specific benefits from a list of choices, such as life insurance or health insurance, to put into a 401(k) plan or to use instead of a 401(k).

Capital Gains Tax: A tax levied on the profit made from selling any "capital" (i.e. non-inventory) asset.

Certificate of Deposit (CD): Certificates issued by banks in exchange for a cash deposit, which is held for a certain period of time and a set interest rate. A bank pays the CD holder the principal amount and all accumulated interest once the specified time period is over.

Compound Interest: Interest on money that accrues on both principal and accumulated interest.

Commission: Fee paid to an agent or insurance salesperson as a percentage of the policy premium. The percentage varies widely depending on coverage, the insurer and the marketing methods.

Consumer Price Index (CPI): The percent change in costs of consumer goods and services. CPI is a metric of consumer-felt inflation, measuring how far your dollar goes towards buying common goods and services. Typically increases 1-3 percent per year.

Contract Owner: The person or entity that makes application for and buys a life insurance or annuity contract. This party is responsible for funding the life insurance or annuity. An owner could be an individual, couple, partnership, corporation, or trust.

Contract Value: The contract value is the total of paid premiums and earnings, less any charges, withdrawals, or fees that may apply.

Chronic Illness Rider: This benefit rider allows the policy owner to accelerate the death benefit if the insured becomes chronically ill. Chronically ill is defined as being unable to perform two of the six activities of daily living (bathing, continence, dressing, eating, toileting and transferring) without assistance from another person, or being severely cognitively impaired for at least 90 consecutive days.

Cost Basis: This is the principal or investment you receive **before** any returns on your cash life insurance, IRA, etc. For example, if you receive $12,000, but originally invested $10,000 then the $10,000 would be the cost basis and $2,000 would be your (ROI) return on investment.

Custodian: The institution or individual holding the assets of another. For example, a custodian may be a bank that holds the assets of a corporation or mutual fund, or it may be an adult who is responsible for the financial activities of a minor child.

Death Benefit: The life insurance or annuity benefit paid to a designated beneficiary when the life insurance or annuity contract's owner dies.

Deferred Annuity: An annuity that provides a way to accumulate monies tax-deferred.

Deferred Compensation: Compensation for services rendered provided under an agreement stating that such compensation will be paid sometime in the future, after the actual services have been performed.

Discretionary Income: The amount of money from income that remains after an individual pays essential bills, such as food, housing, and taxes.

Diversification: The allocation of assets to several different types of investments so as to reduce the risks associated with any single investment, the idea being that losses in one area would be offset by gains in another.

Dividend: A portion of the net profits of an organization that its board of directors allocates for distribution to shareholders.

Durable Power of Attorney: A power that allows you to name someone to manage your financial affairs if you are unable to do so.

Duration: Timeframe of an annuity contract: 1, 2, 3, 5, 7, or 10 years. The longer the duration, the better the return rate on fixed **annuities**.

Employee Retirement Income Security Act (ERISA): The federal law that formed the basis for modern pension regulation by establishing requirements for nondiscrimination, vesting, participation, reporting and disclosure, as well as standards for funding and fiduciary responsibilities.

Endorsement: An addition written to an insurance policy that includes provisions superseding those of the original policy. It is also known as a rider.

Endowment: An insurance policy that pays out its face amount to the individual insured when it reaches maturity, if that person is still alive. If the insured has died before the policy matures, the face amount is paid to a designated beneficiary.

Estate Planning: Planning for the orderly handling, disposition and administration of assets that are left behind after an individual's death. It includes drawing up a will, setting up trusts and figuring out ways to minimize estate taxes.

Equity Indexed Annuity: A type of fixed annuity that earns interest connected to an outside equity index, such as the S&P 500 (Standard & Poor's 500 Composite Stock Price Index).

Equity Vehicle: Investments involving ownership of company stock, futures, commodities, or real estate. Profit in equity vehicles results from their sale after appreciation (growth in value).

Estate Planning: Refers to the preparations made for the administration and disposition of an individual's property either before or after his or her death. Plans may include the creation of wills, trusts, and gifts.

Estate Tax: A tax levied on the net value of the estate of a deceased person before distribution to the heirs.

Executor: An individual named in a will who is designated to carry out the wishes of the deceased person for the distribution of his or her property and who performs this activity under the supervision of a court.

Executor Fees: Fees paid to an individual named in a will who is designated to carry out the wishes of the deceased person for the distribution of his or her property and who performs this activity under the supervision of a court.

Fiduciary: An individual or organization that exercises control over a pension plan and/or the assets it holds.

Fiscal Year: The period of 365 days that is used for purposes of accounting and taxation. It is not necessarily the same period as a calendar year.

Fixed Annuity: An **annuity** contract that provides a guaranteed minimum interest rate and a higher current interest rate for shorter time periods during a deferred annuity's accumulation phase.

Flexible Premium Adjustable Life Insurance Policy: Also called Universal Life type policies.

Forced Annuitization: The mandatory liquidation of an annuity and dispersion of funds, triggered by the death of the annuitant, or if the annuitant reaches a certain maximum age.

Free Look Provision: The provision in a life insurance or annuity contract stating that the owner of the contract has between 10 and 20 days to review the contract immediately after buying it. It gives the buyer the chance to return the contract to the insurer for a total refund and is governed by state regulations, which may vary.

Free Withdrawal Provision: The provision in an annuity contract that allows the owner to withdraw some part of its face value, without the imposition of a withdrawal charge, during the accumulation period.

Grace Period: - The length of time (usually 31 days) after a premium is due and unpaid during which the policy, including all riders, remains in force. If a premium is paid during the grace period, the premium is considered to have been paid on time. In Universal Life policies, it typically provides for coverage to remain in force for 60 days following the date cash value becomes insufficient to support the payment of monthly insurance costs.

Guaranteed Interest Rate: The minimum interest rate an insurer will credit during an annuity contract's accumulation phase, usually between 3 and 4 percent.

Guaranteed Renewable: A policy provision in many products which guarantees the policy owner the right to renew coverage at every policy anniversary date. The company does not have the right to cancel coverage except for nonpayment of premiums by the policy owner; however, the company can raise rates if they choose.

Immediate Annuity: An annuity contract that begins its payout immediately or within a year.

Income Fund: A type of mutual fund designed to provide current income instead of capital growth. Such funds frequently include bonds as other fixed-income holdings.

Index: A statistical system that measures and tracks the performance of similar investments as a group.

Indexed Universal Life: uses an index crediting formula to produce a yield based on policy values.

Indexed Annuities: Uses an index crediting formula to provide a yield on funds inside an annuity.

Individual Retirement Account (IRA): A personal retirement account set up by an employed person with a contribution of up to $2,000 a year (or $4,000 for a couple). Contributions may be tax-deductible, and earnings are not taxed until the funds are withdrawn at age 59½ or later. Variants are the Simple IRA and Roth IRA (see definitions below).

Inflation Risk: This is the risk that inflation may undermine the performance of investments and reduce the future real value of any investments after inflation has been taken into consideration.

Inflation: The loss of purchasing power due to a general rise in the prices of goods and services.

Initial Interest Rate: The rate of interest that is applied to the first deposit made to a fixed, deferred annuity, with the length of time this rate is guaranteed specified in the annuity contract

Interest: Fees paid by banks, entities that issue bonds, and other financial institutions for the use of money provided on loan.

Interest-Crediting Methods: There are at least 35 interest-crediting methods that insurers use. They usually involve some combination of point-to-point, annual reset, yield spread, averaging, or high water mark.

Joint Owner: An individual who co-owns a life insurance or annuity contract with another person. Both have the right to make and approve decisions relating to the contract.

Life Annuity: An annuity that pays a set amount on a regular, periodic basis, for the duration of the annuitant's life.

Liquidity: The ability to quickly convert assets into cash by an individual or organization without incurring significant losses of value.

Living Trust: A legal document that, like a will, contains your instructions for what you want to happen to your assets when you die. Unlike a will, a living trust avoids probate at death, gives you control over all your assets, and prevents the court from controlling your assets if you become incapacitated.

Long Term Care:-is a variety of services that help meet both the medical and non-medical needs of people with a chronic illness or disability who cannot care for themselves for long periods of time.

Long Term Care insurance: A form of supplemental indemnity coverage designed to pay for Long term care expenses in the United States.

Long Term Care rider: A rider provided or purchased within a life insurance or annuity contract that provides benefits for qualified Long term care Events

Maturity Date: The date on which an annuity starts to make income payouts.

Modified Endowment Contract (MEC): If the cumulative premium payments exceed certain amounts specified under the Internal Revenue Code, the life insurance policy will become a Modified Endowment Contract (MEC). Taxation under a MEC is similar to taxation under an annuity. Under a MEC, the death benefit payable to the beneficiary is not subject to income tax.

Medicaid: The federal government health care plan for the financially indigent population of the US.

Medicaid Planning: The practice of attempting to qualify for Medicaid in order to address LTC expenses.

Medicare: The name of the government sponsored health-care plan for those who qualify and apply after the age of 65. It provides very little in the area of LTC benefits.

Medicare Supplement Insurance: An insurance plan that is designed to supplement Medicare coverage for those over 65.

Multi Level Marketing (MLM): Direct Sales or Network Marketing Companies that provide home based business opportunities.

Money Market: Refers to the market for very liquid and low-risk short-term assets, including Treasury bills and negotiable Certificates of Deposit.

Municipal Bonds: A security issued by or on behalf of a local authority.

Mutual Fund: An account combining the funds of many individuals in order to invest these funds in a range of financial instruments. A financial service company usually establishes this type of account.

Net Worth: Add up all your assets, which is what you have and own, then subtract your liabilities, such as debt. The result is your net worth. it's really just one statistic of many that can help you track your financial progress. But it does give you a big-picture view of your financial health.

Non-Qualified Plan: A pension plan that does not meet the requirements for preferential tax treatment. This type of plan allows an employer more flexibility and freedom with coverage requirements, benefit structures, and financing methods.

Participation Rate: Also called the Index Rate, this refers to the part of the index's increase credited to an equity-indexed annuity's account value. In some contracts, a cap is imposed on this amount.

Payout Period: The period of time during which an annuitant is provided payments from an immediate annuity plan.

Pension Plan: A qualified plan designed to provide payments to an employee upon retirement. Pension plans comprise a yearly funding commitment from employers, no access to plan funds before retirement, and restrictions on investments in employer stock to 10 percent.

Period Certain: An income option in an immediate annuity plan whereby the owner of the annuity contract may choose to receive periodic payments for a set period of time, with the payout amount determined by the contract's value and the length of the period of time chosen.

Point-to-Point: A way of calculating index annuity yield. The total yield is simply the difference in index value from the day the annuity is purchased to the day it expires.

Policy Loan: The act of borrowing funds from inside the cash value build up of a life insurance policy.

Policy Owner: The person who owns a life insurance policy. This is usually the insured person or policyholder, but it may also be a relative of the insured, a partnership or a corporation.

Premium: The amount of money paid by the insured in order to maintain their policy.

Primary Beneficiary: The first person named in the policy as beneficiary.

Power Curve: Credit card debt, high taxation, and bad information all work in tandem against your financial goals.

Portfolio: A group of investments considered a unit.

Power Of Attorney: Authorization of one person to make legal decisions and take other actions -- such as signing legal documents -- on behalf of another person.

Premium Bonus: Additional funds that are credited by an insurer to an annuity, expressed as a percentage of the deposited amount.

Premium Tax: Refers to a separate tax imposed on premiums for life insurance or an annuity plan by state governments. While not all states impose this tax, those that do may have different regulations for qualified and non-qualified programs.

Principal: The total amount of money that an annuity contract owner has put into the annuity, excluding earned interest.

Probate: The legal process through which the court sees that, when you die, your debts are paid and your assets are distributed according to your will.

Prospectus: A written document that must be provided under federal regulations to the prospective buyer of a variable annuity before the actual sale. The document describes the investment goals of accounts, past performance of any sub-accounts included, and defines fees and other expenses.

Qualified Annuity: A type of annuity bought with the intention to fund or distribute money from a tax-qualified plan, generally with paid premiums reducing current income tax and the use of tax-deferred accumulations.

Qualified Plan: A private retirement plan that meets the rules and regulations of the Internal Revenue Service. Contributions to such a plan are generally tax-deductible; earnings on such contributions are always tax sheltered until withdrawal.

Reciprocal Tax Formula: A mathematical formula that allows one to see the amount of taxes we pay to earn a dollar.

Retirement planning: The process of determining retirement income goals and the actions and decisions necessary to achieve those goals. Retirement planning includes identifying sources of income, estimating expenses, implementing a savings program and managing assets.

Revocable Living Trust: An alternative to a will that avoids probate and lets you keep control of your assets while you are living, even if you become incapacitated, and after you die.

Rollover: Refers to the monies from a qualified retirement plan or IRA (Individual Retirement Account) that is shifted from one plan to another plan of the same kind, maintaining the tax-deferred status of the funds.

Return on investment (ROI): Is the concept of an investment of some resource yielding a benefit to the investor. A high ROI means the investment gains compare favorably to investment cost. As a performance measure, ROI is used to evaluate the efficiency of an investment or to compare the efficiency of a number of different investments.

Roth IRA: New in 1998, these IRAs are funded with nondeductible contributions and are not taxed upon withdrawal. Only singles with adjusted gross income of less than $95,000 may make a full contribution (partial contributions may be made up to income of $110,000). Likewise, only couples with income less than $150,000 may make a full contribution, with partial contributions allowed up to $160,000.

Rule of 72: In finance, the rule of 72, the rule of 70 and the rule of 69 are methods for estimating an investment's doubling time. The rule number (e.g. 72) is divided by the interest percentage per period to obtain the approximate number of periods (usually years) required for doubling.

Section 1035 Exchange - This refers to a part of the Internal Revenue Code that allows owners to replace a life insurance or annuity policy without creating a taxable event.

Securities: Securities are any form of ownership that can be easily traded on a secondary market, such as stocks and bonds. It also includes their derivatives, such as futures contracts, options, or mutual funds.

Simple IRA: Savings investment match plan for employees for companies with up to 100 employees. Allows workers to put aside up to $6,000 per year; their employers can choose to match contributions dollar for dollar up to 3 percent of the worker's pay or make an across-the-board contribution of 2 percent to each eligible worker. Employers opting for the 3 percent match can cut it to 1 percent for two out of any five years.

Simplified Employee Pension (SEP): A type of retirement plan in which an IRA (Individual Retirement Account) is used to hold contributions; a simpler alternative to a 401(k) or profit-sharing plan.

Single Premium Policy: A life insurance policy paid for in one single premium rather than in annual premiums over a period of time.

Surrender: To give up a whole life policy. The insurer pays the insured the cash value which the policy has built up if it is surrendered.

Single Premium Immediate Annuity (SPIA): A kind of annuity that may be bought into once and yields periodic payouts (monthly, quarterly, or annually) at the cost of compound interest. Future investments require a new annuity purchase.

Sub-Account: Portion of a variable annuity allocating investment into a specific segment, like a money market account, the S&P 500, mutual funds, or Pacific Basin stocks. The choice of sub-accounts makes up the variable annuity portfolio.

Surrender Charge: - Fee charged to a policyholder when a life insurance policy or annuity is surrendered for its cash value. This fee reflects expenses the insurance company incurs by placing the policy on its books, and subsequent administrative expenses.

Surrender Value: Refers to the amount of money received by a contract owner if the annuity is surrendered and all cash is taken out of it.

Surviving Spouse: The term used to describe the living spouse of a deceased plan participant. Under a Qualified Domestic Relations Order (QDRO), a former spouse may be considered a surviving spouse.

Tax-Deductible: An amount of money deducted from the adjusted gross income of a taxpayer in order to calculate the total of taxable income. Medical expenses, paid mortgage interest, and charitable contributions itemized on Schedule A of federal income forms are examples of tax-deductible expenses.

Tax-Deferral: Refers to the fact that earnings from an annuity are not taxed until they are withdrawn from the plan.

Tax-Deferred Income: A feature whereby interest income on an investment is not taxable until the income is withdrawn. This allows for triple compounding: earning interest income on the original principal, interest on the interest earned, and interest on the money you would have paid in taxes.

Term Life Insurance: Life insurance that provides protection for a specified period of time. Common policy periods are one year, five years, 10 years or until the insured reaches age 65 or 70. The policy doesn't build up any of the non forfeiture values associated with whole life policies.

Treasuries: A term that refers to all of the federal government's negotiable securities. Treasury bills (T-bills) have short-term maturities of three and six months and do not pay interest. Instead, they are sold at face value. Treasury bonds may be obtained in $1,000 units and have maturities of ten years or more. Treasury notes have medium-term maturities of between one and ten years.

Underwriting: The process of selecting risks for insurance and classifying them according to their degrees of insurability so that the appropriate rates may be assigned. The process also includes rejection of those risks that do not qualify.

Universal Life: A flexible life insurance policy under which the policyholder may change the death benefit from time to time (with satisfactory evidence of insurability for increases) and vary the amount or timing of premium payments. Also has a cash value account which acts as a sort of savings account that builds interest and can be borrowed against.

Variable Annuity: A kind of annuity contract that allows the owner to allocate the premium amount among several invest-ments, or sub-accounts. The contract value of such a plan may vary according to the performance of these investments.

Variable Life Insurance: A form of life insurance whose face value fluctuates depending upon the value of the dollar, securities or other equity products supporting the policy at the time payment is due.

Vesting: The term used to describe an employee's gaining of the right to be paid a current or future benefit from a pension plan.

Waiver of Premium: A provision in some insurance contracts which enables an insurance company to waive the collection of premiums while keeping the policy in force if the policyholder becomes unable to work because of an accident or injury. The waiver of premium for disability remains in effect as long as the ensured is disabled.

Whole Life: The Life Insurance Industry's first cash value product it is the genesis of all cash value life products in existence today. Whole Life Products provide contractual guarantees which are built into the policy and pricing of the coverage. Whole Life policies often pay dividends as opposed to interest.

Withdrawal Charge: A penalty imposed by the insurer if the contract owner cashes out part of the annuity prematurely. Withdrawal charges typically phase out according to a schedule, e.g., 10 percent before 3 year, 5 percent after 4 years, 0 percent after 5 years. Withdrawal charges may be waived in the event of death or illness.

Yield: This usually refers to the profit amount obtained on a capital investment and also the income portion of the return from a security.

Zero Percent Tax Bracket: The practice of planning for future tax avoidance, where the ultimate goal is to eliminate or drastically reduce taxes during retirement years.

RESOURCES

Preface.
p. 2 -- George Carlin quotation June 24, 2008 "The Real Owners of America."

Chapter 1.

p. 7 -- Edward "Ted" Siedle online article March 20, 2013, titled "the Greatest Retirement Crisis in American History" Forbes.com.

p. 8 -- Excerpts from "The American Income Crisis" by David Malpass, Forbes, September 2, 2013.

p. 9 -- Illustration source Baloocartoons.com 2008.

Chapter 2.

p. 16 -- Quotation from the *"The Richest Man in Babylon"* by George Samuel Clason, 1926.

p. 16 -- Quotation from Supreme Court Justice Louis D. Brandeis 1919-1939, "If I Went over the Toll Bridge."

p. 18 – Illustration from Met Life Mature Market Institute, Transitioning into Retirement, figure 1, 2012.

Chapter 3.

p. 22 -- The average American's absolute minimum tax rate is 59.7 percent or more when you take into account all the taxes and fees estimated as of 2013 at www.nowandfutures.com.

p. 23 -- Illustration from, http://henrymakow.com/the-irs-internal-reality-service.html

Chapter 5.

p. 37 -- Roughly 600,000 people die each year in the prime of their lives. http://www.lifehappens.org/life-recognizes-excellence-in-client-service-with-its-reallifestories-program/

Chapter 7.

p. 55 -- The average fixed indexed annuity pays 13 times more than a one-year jumbo CD and almost four times more than a five year jumbo CD! http://www.bankrate.com/finance/cd/rate-roundup.aspx#ixzz2cqkgoHKi

Chapter 9.

p. 77 -- Little man carrying the tax burden, illustration from Guy Fawkes' Blog.

p. 78 -- Inflation rat illustration obtained from www.truthdig.com.

p. 78 -- "From 1914 until 2013, the United States Inflation Rate averaged 3.35%." www.usinflationcalculator.com/inflation/historical-inflation-rates/.

p. 80 -- Tax cut Illustration obtained from: www.triplepundit.com

p. 89 -- Retirement study by Wharton School at the University of Pennsylvania in August, 2012.

Chapter 10.

p. 99 -- Tuition Inflation chart from: http://www.aidemocracy.org/

p. 102 -- LTC Nationwide Financial Survey. Boomers Planning for Retirement Underestimate Long-Term Care Costs Nationwide. com

p. 105 -- -Gold vs. dollar chart obtained from: http://www.sgmmetals.com/GoldvsUSDollar.aspx

p. 114 -- Retirement Buckets illustration by Raymond Leeper

Chapter 12.

p. 126 -- Why we need a will and regular updates http://money.msn.com/retirement/5-celebrities-who-messed-up-their-wills

ABOUT THE AUTHORS

Barry is a trained electrical engineer, and has over 10 years serving hundreds of clients in the life, health, and retirement insurance business. His previous experience includes more than 25 years managing telecommunications operations in the United States, Latin America, Europe, Africa, and the Middle East.

In addition, he is also the author of "A Manager's Guide to Guerrilla Warfare," "Guess Who's Listening at the Other End of Your Telephone," "The Islamic Conquest of Europe 2020," and Helena, Texas "The Toughest Town on Earth."

As an author, he has been featured in articles or news stories by the Associated Press, LaSoir (Brussels, Belgium), Dallas Times Herald, the Houston Post and Success Magazine to name a few. He has conducted business training seminars and been interviewed on television and talk radio shows across America and Europe.

During the Vietnam Period, Barry served in the United States Naval Air Force as a Combat Air Crewman. Barry is a former kick-boxer, and has five children.

Author Raymond Leeper has been a licensed insurance agent since 1987. Along with his father Paul Leeper (1938-2012) and brother Dale Leeper, he was one of the founding partners of the Leeper Group LLP. Raymond started working when he was 14 years old. He graduated from James Madison High School in San Antonio, Texas.

For the past 24 years he has developed his expertise in the life insurance industry. As a second-generation life insurance professional, Raymond, along with his brother Dale, apprenticed under their father's guidance. Over his tenure as an agent he has helped thousands of individuals and families save and receive millions of dollars in benefits.

His unique understanding of life insurance and, financial and tax strategies could be learned only through his 24 years of experience as an apprentice to Paul Leeper. He has frequently been interviewed by the media as an expert in the area of healthcare reform, tax, and retirement planning.

In addition to his business activities as a founding partner of the Leeper Group LLP, Raymond has been married for 18 years to his wife Veronica. Together they are the proud parents of three children, Estee, Kathleen, and Paul. He is civically active in his local community and an avid golfer. He has resided in San Antonio, Texas, since 1972. Raymond serves with his brother Dale as advisory board members to the Alamo Breast Cancer Foundation, a worldwide-recognized non-profit organization, they helped found in 1994.

www.ingramcontent.com/pod-product-compliance
Lightning Source LLC
Chambersburg PA
CBHW071849200326
41519CB00016B/4301